MW01254422

Enjoy!
Alison M Holst

A Home-grown Cook

The DAME
ALISON HOLST
STORY
with Barbara Larson

HYNDMAN PUBLISHING

Published by Hyndman Publishing
325 Purchas Road
RD 2 Amberley 7482
www.hyndman.co.nz

The moral rights of the authors have
been asserted.

ISBN: 1-877382-67-1

TEXT: © Alison Holst & Barbara Larson

DESIGN: Rob Di Leva

PRINTING: Southern Colour Print

First published 2011

Thanks to *Australian Woman's Weekly*
for the cover image.

Photographs are from the Holst family
collection unless otherwise credited.
The potters of the ceramics pictured on
pp 162 and 223, and the source of the
cartoon on p 112 are unknown.

The quote on p. 19 is from *Coal Range
and Candlelight: Women of Methven and
Districts*.

Acknowledgements

I would like to thank my husband Peter, the rest of my family and the many friends who have supported me in the completion of this book.

I am very grateful to Neil Hyndman, who brought 'a home-grown cook' to life, and to Barbara Larson and Rob Di Leva who encouraged me, edited and designed this work.

Jane Ritchie deserves special mention for her many years of help. She remembered many things I had forgotten over the years!

Alison Holst

I'm grateful to Alison's friends and family who agreed to be interviewed. Special thanks to my dear friends Effin Older and Emma Neale; to Jane Ritchie, Cliff Josephs and Sharon Crosbie; to Patricia Payne and David Galloway; to Clare and Ian Ferguson; and to Kirsten, Simon and Peter Holst.

Thanks to Neil Hyndman for his generosity and faith, and to Rob Di Leva for his grace and patience.

Lastly, a big thank you to Alison for always being herself.

Barbara Larson

Contents

9   Foreword

12   Introduction

Chapter **one:**
15   My Family

Chapter **two:**
29   Our Home on Blacks Road

Chapter **three:**
45   Elbow Room

Chapter **four:**
57   'Here's How'

Chapter **five:**
71   San Francisco Opens Her Golden Gate

Chapter **six:**
87   On the Move

Chapter **seven:**
105   Lemnos Avenue

118 Changing Styles

Chapter **eight:**

121 Four-legged and Feathered Friends

Chapter **nine:**

131 Have Frypan, Will Travel

Chapter **ten:**

145 From Kitchen to Pantry

Chapter **eleven:**

159 Cakes and Quilts

Chapter **twelve:**

175 Life's a Beach

197 All Time Favourite Recipes

Appendix **one:**

224 Margaret Payne's Memoirs

231 100 Cookbook titles

I dedicate this book to the memory of my mother
and father, who I'm sure are looking down at me,
smiling and saying, 'that's nice dear'.

Foreword

Dame Alison Holst not only taught us all how to cook, but how to be adventurous with it. For nearly half a century, she helped change the way New Zealanders eat and prepare food for their families. We trust her culinary judgement and her recipes. Not for her the shouting, cursing and sobbing of contemporary television chefs and hapless budding 'Masterchef' contestants. Her approach is one of warmth and charm and unflustered conviction.

But there is so much more to Alison. She has a rare gift, that of true friendship, and a funny, larky side that her public rarely sees, I suspect. She also lives what she believes: the importance of family and friends, loyalty and kindness. No one who ever rang her at home with a tale of woe and a collapsed cake was turned away; try that with Gordon Ramsay!

Alison is also single-handedly responsible for raising millions of dollars for Plunket and other deserving causes with her famous 'dems'. For decades she travelled to town and country halls throughout New Zealand, often on back roads in the dead of winter, performing culinary miracles with an electric frypan, a sharp knife and her imperturbable good nature.

It has been a privilege to be her friend. We really got to know each other in the radio studio. She allowed me great latitude in our interviews

—I liked teasing her and playing the devil's advocate—and she always rose to the challenge. People still remember our 'conversations' and saw her visits to the studio, along with her recipes and wisdom, as one of the highlights of the week on what was then Radio New Zealand's nine to noon slot, as well as our interviews on talkback radio in Wellington.

Who could forget the 'Potato Recipe' leaflet? There were no computers and no internet in those days, so when literally hundreds of people sent their self-addressed envelopes, we were all involved in the endless 'stuffing' of them in the afternoons, and much cursing.

When Alison responded to a desperate plea from a listener who wanted to know how she could feed her family on $47 a week, Alison made news, nationwide, with the most ingenious use of a side of mutton ever devised. Needless to say there was a run on sides of mutton and the price sky-rocketed.

We have spent time together overseas when Alison was promoting our beef and lamb in the USA and when we both found ourselves in London. There's something about being away from New Zealand, being where no one knows or recognises you, that really loosens the inhibitions. I recall that we descended on Harrods astonished that accessories could really cost THAT much and had to revive ourselves with a slab of game pie from the famous food hall, which we hid on our knees in the health food section, and cut up with Alison's Swiss Army knife (she is never without it). We attempted to divert suspicion by sitting smugly in front of glasses of carrot juice.

At Nieman Marcus in Boston we were thrown out of the fur department by a woman who approached us flapping her hands and caroling, 'My, my, you girls do look comfortable,' as she effectively shooed us out. 'What a nice woman,' said Alison, proof that the good among us only expect good from others! I guess our casual attire didn't quite gel with the US$35,000 mink coats.

Alison once said that the mark of good friendship was being able to go to a friend's fridge, look inside, and not shout 'Ewww!' no matter how many furry things lurked there. I am proud that we have that sort of relationship: one that is based on trust and a 'no surprises' policy! She has many friends who must feel as I do. You get such a lift in her company, no matter how rotten everything else is at the time. A rare gift indeed.

Many years ago, a Sunday paper asked a bunch of people what they would do if they won Lotto. I will always remember that Alison said she would see to it that all classrooms would be equipped with a stove so that every child could learn to cook and be self-sufficient in the kitchen. To her way of thinking, this would mean that no matter how difficult their lives became, they could still take care of themselves.

But being able to make nice food is about so much more than just staying alive. Alison's love of cooking and her ability to enthuse and inspire so many of us with her recipes has been a wonderful gift that we can enjoy every day. She, herself, says nothing gives her more pleasure than spotty, food-stained pages in our copies of her books: it's a sign that a recipe has become part of someone's repertoire. It's proof, too, that she continues to be a wonderful part of our lives, a culinary pioneer and a national treasure.

Sharon Crosbie, August, 2011

Introduction

I have never considered myself to be anything other than a home cook. Initially I set out to teach young mothers how to cook tasty, healthy meals for their families. That's what I most wanted to do. Everything else seemed to just happen. It had never occurred to me to write a book – this will be my 100th title – nor to appear on television, be

Eggs go American
with Alison Holst
Reporting to you
from San Francisco.

interviewed on radio, and certainly not to

travel overseas to promote New Zealand lamb

and beef, attend speaking engagements, nor

to become a business brand. Somehow, my

working life just happened. And

I've loved it, every minute of it.

Alison Holst, July 2011

My parents' wedding photo: *from left, Alwyn Taylor (Dad's cousin), Kathleen Dickie (Mum's younger sister), Arthur Hollier Payne (my father), Margaret Payne (my mother), Mavis Taylor (Dad's cousin), remaining man unknown, 1936.*

Chapter **One:**

My Family

I was born the year before the start of the Second World War in a small private maternity hospital called El Nido. It was not far from my parents' home. We lived in Opoho, a Dunedin suburb that sits high on the hill overlooking North East Valley and the rolling green hills to the northwest.

My parents, as so often happens, met by chance. My father had been chopping wood when a fragment lodged in his eye. He went to the hospital in Christchurch and the nurse who tended him was my mother. As a child, I thought their first meeting was truly romantic and I realised that if it wasn't for this meeting, I wouldn't have been born. Margaret and Arthur Payne married in 1936, then moved to Dunedin when my father was offered a teaching position at the Dunedin Teachers' College.

My mother's full name was Margaret Ardagh Ursula Dickie. Ardagh was the name of the family farm, and Ursula means 'She-bear'. The four initials were important neither: M.A.D. nor M.U.D. was suitable. Margaret was the fifth of seven children and grew up on a farm in Canterbury, near Methven. Mum loved farm life. She'd often regale us with stories from her childhood: the many pet animals they kept, the steady stream of visitors, the never-ending bustle in the kitchen. Later, in my teens, I noticed how she'd glow with pleasure whenever a large number of friends and family gathered around the table to enjoy yet another delicious roast meal followed, of course, by one of her much-loved puddings.

Margaret's mother, Kate Thurza Peyman, was born in 1870 at Herne Bay in Kent, England. Kate lost her mother when she was only three years old so she spent most of her childhood in London with a relative, a seamstress, who was one of the Queen's dressmakers. She taught Kate to sew.

When she was 19, my grandmother bravely sailed to New Zealand. She'd been persuaded by her brothers, who with an uncle, ran a dairy farm in Cobden, near Greymouth. Initially, these two men had been drawn to the West Coast by the lure of gold, but farm life demanded home help — hence the invitation. I'm in no doubt that the contrast between London and Cobden presented a real challenge to the young Kate, but we're told she loved the wild West Coast landscape with its unruly bush and numerous native birds. Kate worked hard and learned a great deal about her new home. (During that time, whitebait was so plentiful it was used as manure!)

My grandmother would often recall the Brunner Mine disaster of 1896 when she, along with others, waited to identify the bodies of the miners. She assisted with the making of shrouds for their burial and with comforting the bereaved. (Sixty-five miners were lost in this tragedy.) And she told my mother of the Grey River floods that were so disastrous that much of Cobden was claimed by the sea.

It was in Cobden that Kate met her future husband, William Dickie. Against her family's wishes, they married in 1896. Perhaps there were

My mother's family. From left, back row: Beacon, Nell, Colin. Middle row: William James Dickie, Kate Thurza Peyman Dickie and Alan. Front row: My mother, Margaret, and her sisters, Kathleen and Heruini.

some questions over William's suitability, but my mother always claimed it was because the family knew Kate's skills would be sorely missed on the farm. The newly married couple moved to Canterbury and started up their own farm, where Kate planted her first garden. Sadly, this farm was subsequently sold, much to the disappointment of my grandmother, but after a few years, William, in partnership with a relation, purchased the Ardagh Estate.

William had the 'gift of the gab', which helped when he later became involved in local affairs. He was elected a member of Parliament for Selwyn in 1911, a role he embraced with gusto. My mother later wrote:

Dad's entry into Parliament for the Selwyn electorate gave him eight busy years – busy ones for mother, too, as she had to cope with us and the farm, while he was engaged in parliamentary business in Wellington. I remember that old Dick Seddon was a household name to us. He was a West Coaster, too, and he and Dad were not unlike one another in appearance. Big burly men they were, and generous to the umpth degree.

My mother's family home, Ardagh, where she was born. It was an 800 acre farm at Lyndhurst.

Table set for a wedding feast in the barn at Ardagh. The neatly piled wheat sacks next to the wall were used for seating.

Threshing machines at Ardagh, my grandparents' farm.

Theirs was a busy and industrious farm. It astonishes me to think that my grandmother, with seven children, would have nine people sitting around the table at every meal, not counting the farm workers who ate in the house as well. The Dickie household has been described as being 'warm and welcoming, with farm employees treated as family'. Ardagh was widely renowned for being an open house to all and a place where wandering swaggers knew they would be offered food and a place to 'doss down' for the night.

Kate was a staunch church-goer, an Anglican, as was my mother. The church was not only the centre of their spiritual lives but also the core of their social world. Music, which they performed themselves, was the mainstay of their entertainment. Singing in the church choir and around the piano at Ardagh on Sunday nights was one of my mother's greatest pleasures.

When the Selwyn seat was abolished in 1919, William lost his parliamentary role after eight years of service. He stood in the Ashburton electorate but was defeated. Sadly, this was the start of his undoing. Again, from my mother:

> *Politics are dicey things though and a person is all to the fore one minute, and when defeated in an election, it was difficult and one was forgotten — so were all the kindnesses which had been shown. Dad was never the same after his defeat in the Ashburton electorate.*

Predictably, this idyllic rural homestead ran into hard times during the Depression. Ardagh suffered financial difficulties, as did most farms at that time, and it seems clear that William fell into a deep melancholy: now we'd call it depression. One day, when everything became too much for him, he quietly slipped into the summer house and shot himself in the head. His suicide was kept a family secret and was never mentioned: his death was referred to as 'untimely'.

I can only guess at the immense grief that my mother must have suffered; she was thirteen when her father died. My grandmother was left with seven children to look after; she was also struggling with a farm that was on the verge of bankruptcy. After a few more hard years, she and her children were eventually forced 'to walk off the farm'. That was when the family moved to Methven.

My grandmother weathered her misfortunes with a wonderfully

robust spirit. She hiked up her skirts and set about developing a new home and garden with the help of Allan, her third son, and her daughters, Margaret, Kathleen and Heruini. The eldest three children had married and left home by this time.

Kate was a warm and ebullient woman and up until about 20 years ago, people would come up to me and say, 'I knew your grandmother, Kate Dickie. She was a wonderful woman. You'd never forget her.' She died a year after I was born.

My grandparents' headstone at Methven cemetery.

Mum, ever her mother's daughter, proved to be a determined young woman. After a short stint at teaching, she went on to study nursing, passing her state examination in 1932. She was an excellent nurse and was awarded the inaugural Bertram E. Hamilton Prize at Christchurch Public Hospital for 'showing the highest degree of essential nursing qualities'.

Dad had a completely different upbringing from Mum. His parents, Alice and Arthur Payne, were born in Canterbury—Arthur in Rangiora and Alice in Christchurch. Their families had emigrated here during the 1860s and seventies. Arthur's mother, Eliza Dorling, was the daughter of a London-based jeweller and his father was a soapmaker from Birmingham.

Dad's parents married in 1904; unfortunately we know very little about their courtship and early life together. Dad was an only child, although he had a brother who tragically died when very young. Their comparatively small family lived quietly in a neat and tidy house in Rangiora. My grandfather ran a brewery while my grandmother stayed at home and looked after the house and garden.

Dad was a scholarly student; he attended Rangiora High School, where he was dux. He went on to study at the University of Canterbury, graduating with a first class honours degree in Geology. He was as much at home with science as with the arts; he hoped for an academic career within the university.

The brutality of the Depression, however, had deeply affected him. He worried about money and security — a clear indication that life must have been hard for the Payne family as well. Once, Dad had to borrow ten pounds and you'd have thought it was the end of the world.

He joined the staff of the Teachers' College in Dunedin soon after he graduated, when the college first opened its doors. He lectured in geography, which was not his chosen field, but he was pleased to have secure work. He later gained a degree in geography also. Dad enjoyed the company of his colleagues and worked at the college until he retired.

My father's graduation photo; he graduated with first class honours in Geology from the University of Canterbury in c. 1930.

My mother and father with me aged 3 months, 1938.

My mother Margaret's nursing graduation photo. She's seated first row on the extreme right. (Date probably 1932.)

At first my parents lived in a rented house in Warden Street, Opoho. They decided they liked the area, and with me as a toddler, they soon moved a couple of blocks away, buying a newly built, three-bedroom brick house at the top of Blacks Road. From this sunny spot we could see the weather coming—either blowing in from the south-west or arriving in drifts of sea mist from the north-east. Often the morning sky would be blue with promise but by noon it would change to dark and threatening.

The women in our street were almost like sisters. Many of their husbands were away at war, so they relied on one another, moving freely in and out of each others' homes, talking, laughing, checking up on us children, borrowing a cup of flour, banding together when needed. Times were tough and the shadow of war hung over their close knit community, but I was blissfully unaware of all this. It was a wonderful, safe haven filled with the ease and generosity of these women. I loved it, and so did my mother.

As the women were at home each day, they pinned up each others' hems and showed newly-wed, younger women how to cook—how to bake biscuits or perhaps a special plum sauce using fruit from a neighbouring tree. They were all in the same boat and worked together like a team. Their lives differed from the way we live now; everyone knew everybody else. I could tell you whose house I was in, even if blindfolded, simply by the smells in the various kitchens, for in those days, pots of soups and stews would invariably be simmering on the stove.

Dad in his Home Guard uniform during World War II: he's in the middle of the back row. (He was a tall man: six foot one.)

Although many of the men were away, Dad had flat feet as well as trouble with his eye, so he wasn't eligible for service. I can remember thinking how pleased I was that he could stay and look after us and, instead, be a member of the Home Guard.

My mother, because she was a nurse, would often be called upon to help families in distress, to tend sick children, to stay on, to sit out the night with an elderly parent so a family member could have a decent night's sleep, or to lay out someone who had died. She did these tasks as a matter of course; it was never something she was paid for.

There was a grocer's store at the corner of Blacks and Signal Hill Road where everyone did their shopping and stopped to chat. Mum put everything on 'tick': flour, butter, sugar, cheese, vegetables and fruit. The bill had to be paid at the end of each month and my father would seize the account and study it diligently, usually with his head in his hands, worrying over the size of the bill.

No one in our street had a car: they used the tram. Dad often picked up the meat or fish on his way home from work. At times, he would take the tram to Normanby to buy a couple of rabbits from the butcher, then walk up the steep hill with the rabbits in his leather attaché case. Once home, he'd cut up the carcasses, wrap each piece in bacon, add some chopped onion, and put the casserole in the oven to slowly cook. Dad's rabbit casserole filled the kitchen with warm comfort.

My mother's sister, Heruini, known to us as Aunty Pip or Ini, served as a New Zealand Army nurse in Egypt during the war. We were intrigued by a photograph of her, probably taken in Cairo, sitting on a camel. When Aunty Pip arrived back from the war she had nowhere to go—their mother had died while Pip was overseas—so she came to stay with us. I remember she wasn't well and went straight to bed. I was told to sit on the floor beside her and read a story. This memory is very clear to me because I'd sat down on a bee on the mat and got stung. I can only assume that my mother nursed Aunty Pip back to health. Not much was said about her illness; I was told that she had 'something wrong with her insides'.

Once Aunty Pip was back on her feet, she and my mother worked night shifts in a small private hospital; not that Mum ever told me about this, as she didn't approve of my working when I had a family. They job-shared, certainly not a phrase that was used then, but between the two of them, they organised it so one would be home while the other worked night duty.

My mother's brother, Allan, also came to live with us when he returned from the war. My mother and I went to the railway station to meet him. The night was pitch black, the sparks from the engine lit up the darkness, and I watched as the returned servicemen excitedly poured out of the train.

Uncle Allan had lost a thumb while overseas, something that both horrified and fascinated us children. As luck would have it, he won a returned serviceman's raffle and the land he won turned out to be part of their original family farm at Ardagh—the same land they had lost during the Depression.

It must have been a shock to Dad to suddenly find himself involved with all Mum's brothers and sisters. Her family was very important to her and she welcomed everyone—not only family but friends and strangers alike—into our home. Later, we often wondered just how Dad coped with the hurly burly of the house on Blacks Road.

It was about this time, when I was four years old, that my sister Patricia was born. She was a beautiful, dark-haired little charmer right from the start. She and I became great playmates. Not that we didn't argue and fight as we got older—we did—but all-in-all, we grew up happily together in our noisy, busy home.

There are many family stories about our childhood naughtiness, like the time we broke a precious wedding gift by playing rather vigorously with some lemons, or when we crashed through our bedroom wall while practising our circus act.

On 1 February 1943, my fifth birthday, I started Opoho Primary School. I loved school and enjoyed the other girls in our class, but Judy Ryburn was my special friend. We would often stop at my house on the way home from school for something to eat, then head off down the hill to Judy's house.

Judy's father, Hubert Ryburn, was Master of Knox College, a Theological College and hall of residence situated on the edge of our suburb. The Ryburn family lived in the Master's House, part of the imposing building that I thought was a castle. The rooms had high ceilings with tall windows and dark, wood-panelled walls.

We would climb the stairs and drop pillows on those below, and occasionally we'd tag along behind Judy's older brother and sister, who I thought were wonderful. We loved sliding on trays down the steep, grassy banks outside the building, and best of all, we'd sometimes be taken by Judy's older siblings to the top of the Knox College tower where we'd drop water-bombs onto the path below. It was a very exciting place to play. Judy and I were to become life-long friends.

Our Opoho School only went up to standard two, so I had a year at Normal School in Union Street, a special school for trainee teachers. It was there that I spent a wonderful year with a gifted teacher, Miss Black. These days we'd say she taught us to think 'outside the square'. She took us outdoors to study cloud formations and taught us the names of garden flowers, after encouraging us to bring these from our home gardens. She also taught us much about the natural world and how to form teams and work together. I found her classes endlessly exciting.

It was with some disappointment that I went back to our little school in Opoho the following year. Two extra classrooms had been built to accommodate the growing district. I remember longing for the animated inspiration of my former teacher.

When I was nine years old and Patricia was five, our youngest sister Clare was born. I was very excited about the new baby and was old enough to be able to help my mother. As soon as Clare could sit in a high chair, I'd feed her the same meal every night — a soft-boiled egg, mashed with bread, always with the crusts carefully cut off, and soft butter. I'd then bathe her and put on her nightclothes. Often, during the late afternoons, I proudly wheeled Clare around the neighbourhood in her pushchair. I looked after her as if she were my own baby. ▪

View from the top of Blacks Road, Opoho,
overlooking the valley below and the hills to the
north-west where Peter and I used to climb.

Our house at 100 Blacks Road, Opoho, Dunedin.
My parents bought this house in 1939, a year
after I was born. (This photo was taken recently.)

Chapter **two:**

Our Home on Blacks Road

As children we visited Dad's parents in Christchurch on a regular basis. Both my grandparents suffered from poor health — they had bad hearts — and were sent to bed for about 20 years, for that is what you did then.

As Dad was their only son, we travelled on the train to Christchurch almost every long holiday, and often my father would travel up on the short holidays, too, just to see how they were. It was a long trip; the train left from the stately Dunedin railway station at eight in the morning and didn't get into Christchurch until four or five in the afternoon.

Dad used to settle us in the train first, then dash off up Stuart Street to buy us each a pickled pig's foot from the deli. It was our treat — I still love them. These delicious, smoky morsels would keep me busy, nibbling, at least until Oamaru, sometimes Timaru. Each time Dad ran off to get our treats, we worried ourselves sick that he wouldn't make it back in time and the train would leave without him.

After Clare was born — she was still in a bassinette — we travelled the now familiar route to my grandparents' house in the Christchurch suburb of St Albans. Not long after our arrival, I was startled to find my mother silently weeping as she bathed Clare in a large bowl, a bowl I still own. The poor woman was exhausted, something I understood even then. Looking after two elderly, bed-ridden parents-in-law, along with a new baby, as well as Patricia and me, was proving to be too much.

Dad could often be found outside digging the garden. He grew Jerusalem artichokes, gooseberries and the usual array of vegetables. But even though domestic activities on these 'holidays' took priority, Dad often made time to take us fishing. Patricia and I loved to catch little fish from

Four generations. From left: my paternal grandfather, my great-grandmother holding me, and my father, 1938.

All set for the St Martin's Church Hall parade. Patricia is a little Dutch girl, I'm a fairy and Noelene Tyrel is the blonde fairy on the left.

the banks of the Avon with our fishing nets. Dad also took me on his bike to do the shopping; I sat in front on the well-padded bar.

Breakfast at my grandparents' was my favourite meal: bread and hot milk. It was simply buttered bread, cut in cubes, with hot milk poured over the top. Grandad liked salt and pepper with his; my grandmother preferred sugar. We loved it! Sometimes we'd add chopped parsley — my preference was parsley and sugar. Mum sniffed at bread and hot milk. 'Frightful pap,' she'd mutter under her breath.

Although Mum tired of travelling to Christchurch every summer holiday, she enjoyed visiting her family who lived in the district. Before setting out, Patricia and I dressed up in our matching smocked Viyella dresses, for that is what you wore when you went visiting. Mum of course, had not only made our frocks, she had also smocked the bodice of each.

Later, as my grandparents' health deteriorated even further, my mother and father arranged for people to care for them. At one stage, a couple lived in, greatly easing the burden on my parents.

....

At home we had our own thriving vegetable garden. This was Dad's domain. He had a large, rectangular plot and grew most of our vegetables as well as thyme, sage, parsley and salad greens. We had a few apricot trees and a Peasgood's Nonsuch — a great cooking apple — and a Cox's Orange for eating. Dad loved flowers and grew roses and delphiniums at the front of the house. He planted a lemon verbena beside the path and my mother would pick a sprig of it to give to departing guests.

While my sisters and I were growing up, there was seldom a time when there were no animals at our house. As Mum had grown up surrounded by farm animals she was happy for us to have pets of our own.

With Patricia in her pram, Mum and I often walked to the poultry farm nearby. The hens were friendly and well-cared for and, so I thought,

Three sisters: Patricia, Clare and me with one of our baby rabbits, 1948.

beautiful. Further along was another property that we called in on. The owner, a quiet Japanese man, had large incubators where he placed the hatching chook eggs. A day or so after they hatched, the chicks were sexed; the females were sold, but the young males were given away.

We took several male chicks home to spend their first week in a wooden box in our hot-water cupboard. Mum nailed strips of flannel to the lid of the box so the chicks, according to her, would think they were close to hen feathers and would stay warm and comfortable.

A week or so later, the young chicks were transferred to a hen house built by Uncle Albert, my father's uncle. For a few weeks each year, Uncle Albert came to stay. He built all sorts of things around the house including wardrobes for our bedrooms, a dog kennel, and some years later, a garage for our car.

I wrote a poem about him—perhaps assisted by my mother—that was published in a paper for children:

My uncle Albert came to stay.
He's really old—his hair is grey.
But building things is his delight—
he works all day from morn till night.
He makes us sheds and fixes brooms,
he mends our steps and paints our rooms.
So when his time to leave comes nigh,
we're really sad to say goodbye!

The young roosters enjoyed a happy life for some months until my mother, a farm girl after all, suggested to my father that it was time to 'deal with them'. Every few weeks Dad was urged to go out into the backyard with an axe in hand. As I recall, he seemed to need a fair bit of persuading. I'm sure he was pleased when finally all the birds had been cooked and eaten.

We had hens, too, but as they provided us with a regular supply of eggs, they enjoyed longer lives. The hens had the run of the backyard. (Another of Uncle Albert's projects was a fence around the vegetable garden.) Usually by mid-afternoon, the hens decided it was time to be fed and up the ramp they marched to the kitchen door, jumping onto the handrail and up to the ledge outside the kitchen window. From here they could keep a hungry eye

OPOHO SCHOOL School.
RECORD OF SURVEYS, 1948
Name Alison M. Payne   Class Std. 4

Key to Merit Scale—Ex. 90% - 100%   V.F. 50% - 64%
V.G. 80% - 89%   F. 40% - 49%
G. 65% - 79%   Wk. under 30%

SUBJECT	RECORD 1st	2nd	REMARKS
Art	Ex.	V.G.	1st.
Handwork			Alison is a very
Written Expression	V.G+	Ex.	good worker, keenly
Formal Language	Ex.	V.G.	interested in her
History	Ex.	Ex.	work.
Geography		V.G.	
Reading	G+	Ex.	2nd. Alison has
Spelling	Ex.	Ex.	worked well and
Writing	V.G.	V.G.	shows a better
Arithmetic	G.	Ex.	all round level
Science	Ex.	V.G.	of attainment.
Sewing	V.F.	G+	

Classification for 1949 :   Standard Form I
THE PARENT OR GUARDIAN IS REQUESTED TO EXAMINE THE REPORT AND RETURN IT TO THE SCHOOL.
Initials of Parent or Guardian   N. J. New
Headmaster

on my mother. Their curiosity drove her mad. Often, when I came home from school, I found kitchen trays placed all along the window so the hens couldn't see Mum, and better still, she couldn't see them.

At dusk, it was my job to scoop the hens up into my arms and carry them back to the henhouse. I'd dump the chooks inside and scatter some wheat to keep them happy. In the mornings, Mum mixed a large pot of warm mash, adding porridge and leftover cooked vegetables. I took this rather lumpy brew out to the girls for their breakfast. Because these hens knew me well, they happily sat on my knee and enjoyed being stroked. I loved gathering their warm, toast-brown eggs.

One evening, when I was nine, I answered the front door to find Graeme Johnson, one of the boys in my class from school, standing there. He put his hand inside his jacket pocket and silently handed me a small, baby rabbit, then another from his other pocket. He never said a word —he had probably been sent by his mother—just turned and left. I was thrilled and returned to the living room with this wonderful gift in my cupped hands!

The baby rabbits lived in the wooden chicken-box in the hot-water cupboard for several days. Every morning and night we fed them diluted milk using an eye-dropper, and of course, cuddled and held them close. Soon they grew old enough to be put in a larger cage in the back garden where they ate all the vegetables on offer. We never allowed the rabbits to run around free. We'd seen wild rabbits take off like a shot and were frightened that these little creatures would do the same.

Eventually, the time came when my parents decided that the rabbits should be freed. (We didn't know then what pests they could become.) Full of dread, Patricia and I walked slowly and miserably, as if in a funeral procession, behind our father to the end of Blacks Road. When we opened the cage we expected the rabbits to charge out and escape, but they just sat there. Patricia and I knelt down and began stroking their soft velvety ears. Before long the rabbits perked up and began moving around a bit, nibbling at the grass. At that point, my father picked up the empty cage clearly indicating that it was time to leave our little pets to their own devices. Patricia and I cried loudly all the way home! We never saw our rabbits again.

I can't remember where our very intelligent, striped cat, Teens, came from. He had black and grey tiger-like markings. Although he was not allowed into our beds, he often jumped onto mine waiting for me to lift the covers so he could lie stretched out behind my back: a hot-water-bottle-cat.

It was my job to feed Teens in the morning. I used large kitchen scissors to cut up his raw meat. If he hadn't appeared, I stood outside the kitchen door snapping them loudly. It wouldn't be long before I'd hear him leaping over the backyard fence coming home for breakfast. Often he draped himself around my neck for hours at a time, and if he heard me talking to friends as I walked home from the bus stop, he strolled up the road to meet me. We had this much-loved, delightful cat for many years.

Dad brought home a puppy when I was about ten. We thought he was a cocker spaniel but he grew and grew into a large, exuberant, bouncy springer spaniel that created havoc around the household. All concerned were relieved when Freckles was given away to a young man who wanted a hunting dog.

When I started intermediate school, Dad and I walked down the hill together every morning. It was such a nice thing for

Dad with our much-loved cat Teens.

us to have this quiet time away from the hubbub of home. We walked through the Dunedin Botanic Garden with its splendid azaleas and rhododendrons. Dad then went on to Teachers' College as I walked over the Leith River bridge to school. Our morning walks gave us a chance to talk about all manner of things. He taught me the names of trees and plants and birds, instilling in me an appreciation of the natural world. I suspect we shared a similar temperament.

Later when I was at Otago Girls', Dad and I hiked up Mt Cargill or trekked over to the Organ Pipes; sometimes we went as far as Flagstaff Hill or up the Leith Valley. Mum encouraged these walks; I was lucky, I had quite a lot of Dad to myself. I now believe that my parents tried their utmost to keep me from being overwhelmed by our domestic life.

Dad with his geologist's hammer by the Otago Harbour, c. 1940.

Dad had a talent for drawing. His lines were sure and definite and flowing. With a few strokes he'd capture the shape of a cat and drew cartoons with ease. I admired his skill, doing my best to copy him. Occasionally, on the weekend, he took me to the college and we'd both draw on the blackboard in his lecture room. My drawings would be erased before we left, but his would remain for use on Monday.

My sisters and I were encouraged to attend art classes with the well-known Dunedin artist, Harry V. Miller. He was a lovely, quiet man who taught me how to look at things carefully and to paint with watercolours, something I've come back to in my later years.

Dad on a field trip with his students from the Teachers' College.

H. V. Miller supplied us with paper and paints as well as a new subject each week. I attended his classes for about four years.

From an early age, my mother encouraged me and my sisters to work. She found me babysitting jobs around our neighbourhood. Sometimes I even lived in for two or three nights while the parents were away — I cooked and hung out their washing. I enjoyed babysitting; I liked the peace and quiet after putting the children to bed, and making myself a cup of Milo.

When I was 13, Mum got me a job in Terry's Bookshop. I can just see her walking in and saying to Mr Dixon, 'If you need some extra help, my daughter would do you proud. She's very polite and works hard!' I'm not at all sure he wanted to hire me, but how could he refuse?

Terry's was a popular Dunedin institution with a music store on one side and a bookstore on the other. I worked in the children's section at the back and received ten shillings for my Friday night shifts. To my surprise, I turned out to be quite a good sales person.

TELEPHONE
No. 18-934

Training College,
Union Street,
Dunedin, N.1.

MEMORANDUM

TO   WHOM   IT   MAY   CONCERN:

I have pleasure in testifying to the excellent personal and professional qualities of Mr A.H.Payne M.A., who has been closely associated with me on the staff of the Dunedin Teachers' Training College for the past 15 years as Lecturer in Geography.   During that time I have formed the highest opinion of him as a man and as a lecturer.

Mr Payne holds an M.A. degree with First Class Honours in Geology and has subsequently proceeded to Stage III in Geography.   Mr Payne is deeply attached to his subject and this, together with his undoubted teaching ability and energy, has stimulated and satisfied the interests of his students to a remarkable degree.

His lecturing is reinforced by carefully planned field work and well-organised excursions.

In addition to his normal lecturing programme in Geography, Mr Payne has taken a keen interest in the individual and his tutorials have been most acceptable and valuable to our students.

Mr Payne was somewhat of a pioneer in the field of visual aids and has accepted the responsibility of teaching and demonstrating their use throughout the College.

Mr Payne's extra curricular duties which he has discharged with cheerful readiness and efficiency include the - sponsor-ship of the College Photographic Club, the men's Cricket Club and one of the Rugby Teams.

Mr Payne has wide outside interests.   He acted as first Hon. Secretary of the Otago Branch of the N.Z.Geographical Society, and the success of this venture was largely due to his keen interest and unremitting work.   At present he is the President of the Branch.

Mr Payne is a man of splendid physique and very good personality and address.

His fine personal and professional qualities have earned him the respect and warm friendship of his colleagues.

Jas.W. Armstrong
Principal

My father was a quiet, scholarly man who was highly regarded by his colleagues.

During the quiet times, I'd read. Mr Dixon once caught me reading *Forever Amber* under the counter. He loudly announced, 'If you want to read, there are much better books than this.' I was mortified and red-faced for the rest of the evening.

If someone wished to buy sheet music, 'Old' Mrs Dixon, the owner's white-haired mother, played the piece for them on the piano. Besides sheet music, there were modern pianos, accordions and various musical instruments for sale.

While attending high school, I worked as a nurse-aide at the private nursing home where my mother also worked. When I'd arrive after school, it amused me to find all the old ladies sitting up in bed. I cooked the meals when the cook was away — it was a badly equipped kitchen, but they had lovely china. I used to quickly dish up the food, then run up and down the hallways delivering the meals, hoping they would arrive while still hot.

Mrs Reid, the owner, came up behind me one day while I was busy cleaning someone's false teeth. She gave me such a fright that I dropped the teeth down the sluice — the same sluice where the bedpans were emptied. I had the frightful job of fishing out the lost teeth while fighting back tears and a strong inclination to gag.

Looking back, it didn't do us any harm having to work after school and during the holidays. Money never went far enough and Mum wanted us to be independent and try everything. How else could we find out what suited us best? Most importantly, our parents placed no limits on us because we were girls — they encouraged us and tried their best to give us a well-rounded education. We weren't growled at very much either and although our home life could become a bit chaotic from time to time, it was a wonderfully happy household.

When I was in my early teens Mum ran into an old school friend, Margaret Gilkison. She and my mother had attended the same boarding school in Christchurch. Aunty Margaret, as she became, and her husband Lin had a sheep farm in Southland, situated between Lumsden and Mossburn. This chance meeting changed our lives.

By this time, my father's parents had passed away, so our trips to Christchurch had become infrequent. Aunty Margaret invited our family to their farm during the holidays. She had a big car — it was a time when sheep farmers were doing well — she'd arrive, put us all in the back seat and off we'd go to Lumsden.

Mum loved these visits and was in her element being back on a farm. She'd whip up cream puffs nearly every day for afternoon tea; Mum and Aunty Margaret worked together in the big kitchen with real enjoyment. As there were eleven of us sitting around the table, for every meal, we'd get through a sheep in two or three days.

I learned how to milk from Aunty Margaret's older sons. We'd dump the milk in the separator, and Aunty Margaret would whip the cream in the big Kenwood mixer till it turned to butter. It was my job to make the butter balls for the table.

We went to the farm at different times of the year: depending on the weather, we'd go mushrooming or on camping trips to Te Anau. The camping holidays were elaborate excursions that usually involved the big car, a caravan and a truck. Occasionally we'd drive up to Lake Wakatipu for a picnic. The Gilkison's farm backed onto the Oreti River where we spent many happy hours fishing and swimming in the pools. Dad didn't always come with us to the farm, because he often had geography papers from the University of Otago to mark during the holidays, but when he did come, he enjoyed it too.

At home, on the weekends, we had dinner in the middle of the day. Since we went off to church on Sunday, and Dad, a quiet agnostic, stayed home, it was his responsibility to look after the roast and the vegetables. St Martin's Anglican Church was situated in North East Valley at the bottom of our steep street, and as I've mentioned before, we lived at the top. I had to teach Sunday school—my mother made me—and Patricia sang in the church choir. Her distinctive voice could be heard well above the others. At times I sang in the choir too, but I thought teaching Sunday school was quite enough.

After Sunday school I walked back up the hill to meet my family only to then walk back down again to attend church. We traipsed up and down that blasted hill several times on Sundays. I remember feeling quite annoyed that there weren't any Anglican churches in Opoho. The Presbyterians were well served in our suburb; there were times when I wished we were Presbyterian.

After church we'd have our family roast dinner, then mum and dad would snooze for most of the afternoon in front of the fire. This gave Patricia and me the perfect opportunity to experiment in the kitchen. We'd make fudge and toffee that would sometimes boil over into a sticky mess, but this rarely put us off.

....

M y mother was a very good cook who insisted on us having a cooked breakfast. You couldn't leave the house without eating your porridge first, because you had to have porridge, along with toast and a glass of milk. This was followed by either kidneys on toast, or sweetbreads, liver and bacon, oyster fritters,

Patricia (left) and I wearing matching coats with velvet collars made by a neighbour, Mrs Peart. Photo taken at Blacks Road, 1947.

whitebait fritters, or bacon and eggs. Mum liked us to have something different every morning. While she was cooking breakfast, she was cutting our lunches as well. She sliced the bread—these were the days before you could buy sliced bread—then made each of us six sandwiches and packed two or three homemade biscuits or cakes and a piece of fruit. My mother was very strict about the fruit. The sandwiches always had flair: my sisters and I refer to them today as 'gourmet' sandwiches. We had crayfish on white bread with a spritz of vinegar; oysters in white sauce on brown bread; or a special egg spread with parsley and other herbs from the garden. Our lunches were wrapped up in greaseproof paper and put in paper bags ready for us as we went out the door. Mum didn't ever get to sit down until everyone had gone off to school or work.

She spent a day each week baking; in those days, your cooking was judged not on your meals but on your baking. Mum was so well-known for her baking that when it came to the church cake stalls, she had to enter the hall with her cakes carried high over her head because everyone wanted to buy them before she got in the door.

Mum held afternoon tea parties every few months. That's when she really used to bake... for days. Her guests were usually the wives of my father's colleagues from the Teachers' College, but sometimes there were new arrivals to be welcomed by the neighbourhood. The women were entertained in the 'sitting room' and, still wearing their hats, drank cups of tea from the assorted fine china Mum had collected. Each guest was served from a cup and saucer with a matching plate.

After a suitable amount of chat, the splendid pageantry of delicious afternoon tea would be wheeled into the room on the tea wagon. My mother stood beaming, clearly pleased with the exclamations of delight from her guests. The sandwiches were always daintily prepared, for you only wanted a taste. There were plates of Neenish tarts: pastries with a sweet, creamy, rum-flavoured filling, topped with chocolate icing on one side and vanilla icing on the other. Scones and pikelets were served along with bowls of jam and cream. Meringues were our favourites, but my mother's masterpiece, her sponge cake, always took centre stage. Usually it was piled with cream and whatever fresh fruit the season provided, perhaps a new crop of strawberries or raspberries.

Patricia and I were expected to perform for the ladies. We hated these engagements but had no option but to go along with the rhythms and rituals of the day. Patricia's voice was extraordinarily powerful and she'd belt out a few songs accompanied by my much weaker attempts. I didn't mind too much since my shyness was overshadowed by Patricia's grand presence. With Mum on the piano, we sang 'When Daisies Pied' and 'Lavender's Blue, Dilly Dilly'.

We'd then make a hasty retreat, grabbing a few pikelets on our way out. What topics these women discussed, I'll never know. We were only wheeled in, like the tea wagon, when required. But these occasions made my mother very happy. Probably they reminded her of her childhood on the farm.

Mum loved having people join us for food. We often said, 'Oh Mum, not again. Can't it just be us?' but these requests were breezily waved aside. She'd often bring someone home for dinner, someone she'd just met at church. She'd say, 'You look as if you could use a good hot meal,' and then trot them up the hill to our house.

One of our mother's favourite expressions was, 'If there's enough for five, there's enough for seven.' Patricia claims that 'the kitchen was her stage' and so it would seem. She had hot soup bubbling on the stove, waiting for us, after school. Often we were greeted with the sweet warm smells of baking as we opened the front door. It's no small wonder we grew, and grew some more, into big, tall, strapping girls. By the time I was fully grown, I stood five-foot-ten inches, Patricia reached six feet, and Clare grew to a magnificent six-foot-two. ▪

Patricia, Clare and I in uniform, 1955.

Chapter **three:**

Elbow Room

I attended my very first cooking class while at Dunedin North Intermediate School. Our teacher, Miss Irvine, wore a starched cap and white uniform, and ran the cooking room as if it were her own kingdom — moving about at a brisk pace with great efficiency. Preparing a lemon drink was our introduction to the culinary arts. Why it took us an hour and a half to make, one can only guess, but I proudly took mine home in a bottle to share with my family.

After a year of classes, we were expected to cook a meal for four. Taking this responsibility to heart, I invited my father and one of his colleagues from the Teachers' College for lunch. I can't remember what I served but I do remember feeling quite pleased with the results, and thanks to Miss Irvine, realised, probably for the first time, that cooking could be not only interesting but challenging.

At home, Mum did most of the cooking. Our small kitchen was her domain — we assisted by peeling potatoes and preparing vegetables — and

I discovered early on, that if I set the table straight after school while my mother was out, I could usually sneak off and lie on my bed to read and still earn 'brownie points'.

....

In 1952, after both my paternal grandparents died, my father sold the Christchurch house and was able to buy our first car. This car changed our lives in so many ways. It gave us the freedom to pack up and head off for a picnic on the spur of a moment. Mum had been given a Prestige pressure cooker — a 'mod-con' that she'd embraced and mastered — and she'd take whatever she had in the cooker, usually corned beef or a chicken, put some bread and salad in a basket, and off we'd go.

During the long, summer evenings that the south enjoys, we'd head to Bethunes Gully on a week night, or to Brighton Beach on the southern coast at the weekends. Unfortunately Mum never learned to drive, something she later regretted. As soon as I reached 16, I got my driver's licence. I could then drive Mum to the private hospital where she did night duty and pick her up again at 7 a.m.

As I've mentioned, I attended Otago Girls' High. I enjoyed school and did reasonably well academically. For two years, I was a prefect. I didn't mind the added responsibility; I was quite serious and usually did all the right things. I liked knowing what you were supposed to do, then doing it well. You could have described me as being well-behaved.

I wasn't very sporty, but during the warm weather, I'd rush home from school and play tennis with my friends on the courts beside the Alhambra football ground in Opoho. We had cooking classes at Girls' High, too, but they, like the art and craft classes were less than inspiring. However, I remember making pigskin gloves that I wore for several years. Turning the flat leather into a three-dimensional object held a special appeal.

There were no male teachers at the school. Most of our teachers —

there were exceptions of course—were in their forties and none were married. Later, I wondered if they had lost loved ones during the war. They were nice women, although a few were rather strict; naturally, some stood out from the others. Miss Henderson, our Latin teacher, had eyes in the back of her head, and Miss Chase Clark, our attractive and lively music teacher, inspired us with her enthusiasm. I joined the Special Choir and loved the sound of our four-part harmony reverberating around the empty school hall.

A memorable occasion for me was being one of the girls chosen from all the various secondary schools in Dunedin to sing in a concert put on for the Queen in a packed Town Hall. The Queen's tiara sparkled, her evening dress was beautiful, and we sang very well on the night.

English was probably my favourite subject: the sound and feeling of words have always interested me. To this day, it gives me great satisfaction to write a good sentence and to express myself in a direct manner.

While we were in our teens, Mum insisted that we not only attend church but the church socials as well. I didn't like these occasions—it was humiliating sitting around waiting for someone to ask you to dance. There were always more girls than boys and I wasn't keen to dance with someone shorter than I was.

By the time I left school, I had my heart set on studying architecture. I'm not sure where this preoccupation came from but I loved house-planning. If a house was being built in our neighbourhood, I'd crawl all over it, trying to work out how everything fit together. Studying fine arts also appealed to me, but both courses involved moving to Christchurch, where I would have to stay in a student hostel, and my parents quickly vetoed that idea. According to them, I needed a student-ship, which would bond me to teach for several years. But it also meant that I would be paid an allowance while studying.

My father had been told by a colleague that the Home Science degree

From left: Clare at 11 years old, Patricia at 16 years old and me at 20, 1958.

course at the University of Otago included some design classes as well as house-planning, so this made me feel a bit better, and I was duly enrolled. I felt disappointed at the time, but understood that my parents couldn't afford to send me to Christchurch, so that was that.

Once I started the Home Science course, I enjoyed it. We had to pass medical intermediate, studying the sciences: biology, chemistry and physics. Having young men in our class was a novelty for most of us. The course as a whole was challenging, but it seemed a bit schizophrenic at times — you never knew if you should be studying physics or putting up a hem. However, I liked the variety we were offered, as well as the practical, hands-on approach to things. I enjoyed sewing, as I'd been making my own clothes for several years, but the instruction we received took us to a new, more elegant level. The subject I enjoyed most was cooking.

Our degree class was small: there were ten of us. Looking back on it now, I remember feeling quite lonely and isolated in some ways. My friend Judy Ryburn and I were Dunedin girls so we continued to live at home with our parents. The two of us envied the others who lived in the hostel; to our minds, they appeared to have more fun.

I lived at home for four years while completing my degree; it was during this time that my mother's health was of some concern. Mum, being Mum, would never talk about it, but there were many visits to the doctor, and evidence of excess bleeding, with things being 'not quite right'. She continued being the outgoing person she always had been— inviting people home for tea and talking to everyone in the street. On the face of it, there was no sign of her slowing down.

Home Science wasn't considered to be as difficult as, say, studying medicine, but it was probably more academic than many realised. A subject like 'Laundry' didn't exactly elevate our status, but we made light of this by referring to it as 'Sprinking One' and 'Two'.

My route to university from our home on Blacks Road entailed going through the Botanic Garden. Every morning, as soon as I reached the entrance to the 'Top Gardens', I'd take off my shoes and run for my life through the azaleas, then down through the rhododendrons until I reached the bottom of the hill. Then, I'd slip back into my shoes and walk sedately the rest of the way to class. I loved these early morning runs but more importantly, they helped me get to university faster. I also ran fast because my mother worried about the 'undesirables' who hung around the gardens—and there were some, of course—but they'd have had to run extra-fast to catch me!

In 1960, after four years of study and with my Bachelor of Home Science degree in my pocket, I headed north with three others from my class to spend a year at the Auckland Teachers' College. We were full of the excitement all young people feel when embarking on the brink of a professional career, but unfortunately we found our course less than satisfactory. We weren't assigned a 'proper' lecturer, only a caretaker of sorts: a woman who spent most of her time chatting to us and knitting! Our real training started the minute we were sent out, on section, to teach at various secondary schools.

My assignments couldn't have been more varied: the first was at St Cuthbert's, a private girls' school in Epsom, then next a huge co-ed secondary in an Auckland suburb. I was later sent to Dunedin to teach at my old school, Otago Girls' High, and to King Edward Technical College, which in those days was a very tough school. I spent three to four weeks at each institution and it was in front of these classes that I learned to hold my own and keep the attention of the students.

My three Home Science friends—Judy Ryburn, Gwynneth Turnbull and Beverley Cornish—and I found a villa to rent in Auckland on Onslow Avenue. In fact, it was half a villa: it was divided down the middle into two flats. There was a living room at the front and two small bedrooms and a kitchen and laundry at the rear. We each shared a bedroom; I shared with my special friend Judy.

We walked the half-mile or so to class. Although it rained briefly every day, it was warm, too, and to Judy and me, Auckland seemed delightfully exotic. We had a great deal of fun flatting together. None of us had any money, living as we did off the smell of an oily rag.

We shared the cooking and were surprisingly inventive with the most basic of ingredients. All of us were pretty good cooks; lots of vegetables, and cheap meat-cuts appeared on the menu every night, but our stews, sausages and 50-ways-with mince meant we had plenty of variety. I enjoyed preparing meals with my friends—we laughed a lot in our little kitchen. Occasionally, I would surprise them with a pudding, knowing full well my mother would be pleased.

We certainly didn't live the high life. It was a big deal if we went to the city on the bus. Fortunately we had friends who had cars and they kindly took us to visit some of the many Auckland beaches. Driving through the lush, semi-tropical countryside and swimming in the almost tepid water was a tonic to us southern girls.

I travelled back and forth to Dunedin during the two term breaks, taking the train and ferry: a long, arduous trip, but when you're young these things seem like yet another adventure. The train was certainly cheaper than flying.

It was during one of my visits home that I discovered my mother had been rushed to hospital. She had suffered from colitis for a number of years and now had to have her bowel removed. When I first saw Mum in hospital, I hardly recognised her. It was shattering to see this once vibrant and strong woman so reduced in size that she made barely a bump in the bed. She spent three months in hospital.

Mum and Dad at a family wedding. I've always admired my mother's slim ankles.

Mum's strong character and family support sustained her through this horrible illness. She learned how to manage her disability, and once she recovered, she carried on as if nothing had happened.

Recently a family story came to light, which to my mind, sums up Mum's tremendous energy and selfless drive. According to Patricia, when I was very young, Mum received a message from her sister, Nell, who lived in St Clair on the other side of Dunedin. The message came via a neighbour, since we didn't have a phone at the time: 'I don't think my daughter is at all well and I'm really worried.'

My mother immediately set off for St Clair on the tram. On arrival, she took one look at her 11-year-old niece and called a doctor — one who had apparently been checking the health of young soldiers about to leave for the war. The exhausted doctor pronounced that Margs had flu, prescribing aspirin.

My mother wasn't convinced and asked her sister if she had any money. Nell had some cash and Mum promptly took the child in a taxi to Mercy Hospital where she knew the matron. The poor child was found to have peritonitis and was very ill indeed. The situation became urgent, and the doctor asked if they could test Mum's blood. Fortunately it was the same as her niece's and the child was operated on within the hour. My mother stayed at the hospital to make sure Margs was all right then took the tram back to Blacks Road. Once home, she put on her apron and didn't ever say anything about it to anyone.

Baby Patricia, Kathleen (my mother's sister), Margaret (my mother), Margaret Woodcock (my mother's niece) and me with roses, 1944. Margaret claims my mother saved her life when she was a child.

Peter and I got engaged during the year I was studying in Auckland. We'd met at a Capping Week 'Wool-store Hop' while in our first year at Otago University. We were both a bit shy and didn't meet again until a couple of years later, when I invited him to the Home Science ball. I liked him straight away and I think we knew ours was a special friendship. When we got engaged Peter gave me a ring with a diamond that I still wear.

We had very little money — we were students, after all — but Peter continually thought of interesting things for us to do. We went for long walks on the weekends. Being practical, Peter would have maps and knew exactly where we were going, how long it would take, and without exception, took along something to start a fire. Sherry Pup, Patricia's golden spaniel, came too — did that dog love Peter! He'd carry her in his haversack when she got tired and never forgot a bowl for her water. From the first time I met Peter, he impressed me.

During the year I was in Auckland, I had vague plans to teach science when I finished Teachers' College. However, towards the latter part of the year, Miss Eleanor Gray, who was head of the Foods Department at the Home Science School, wrote to ask if I'd like to apply for a junior lecturer's job in her department, starting in January. I was very excited, but slightly bemused by this invitation, coming as it did out of the blue. The position was an opportunity which I really welcomed, especially as Peter was studying at the Medical School in Dunedin and teaching jobs were hard to come by. I accepted immediately!

My year in Auckland may have been disappointing academically, but

Peter with Teens and Sherry Pup at 100 Blacks Road, Opoho, Dunedin, 1961.

Peter and I on our wedding day. (I made the cake and iced it!)

Our wedding party: from left, Richard Holst (Peter's brother), Clare, Peter, me, John Wattie (Peter's best man) and Patricia. Clare and Patricia were my bridesmaids.

it did give me a bit of elbow room; a pleasant interval between living at home and getting married.

When I first moved back to Dunedin, I lived at home. Saving money was a priority — Peter and I planned to marry during the May holidays — and I had a wedding dress and two bridesmaids' dresses to make, as well as learning how to teach first and second year students in the Foods Department.

On 15th May 1961, Peter and I were married in St Martin's Anglican Church. Patricia and Clare were my lovely bridesmaids, John Wattie was Peter's best man, and Richard, Peter's younger brother, was groomsman. Our reception was held in the Tea Kiosk, in the Botanic Garden, where we had so often walked together. (I'm smiling as I write this, because only yesterday I rang Patricia in Dunedin and Clare in London to remind them that exactly 50 years ago, they had walked up the aisle in St Martin's Church at our wedding.)

On our honeymoon, Peter and I rented a little car and took off for a camping trip. We were on Cloud Nine! We drove through the Haast Pass and on to Central Otago. Peter had packed everything we needed and we camped in secluded bush clearings and beside beautiful, rushing rivers. It was autumn and the poplar trees were turning gold. Frosts and sand-flies didn't bother us. We couldn't have been happier in our small tent.

Peter is such an important part of my life that I can't imagine being without him. Of course we have our moments — but I love him to bits and am full of admiration for him. I met Peter, and ever since, he has been the love of my life.

On the set with 'Here's How', my first TV series, filmed in Dunedin. Late sixties.

Chapter **four:**

'Here's How'

Peter and I started our new life together in a flat on Albany Street. It was close to the hospital and the university, which suited us both. The rent was perfect: it cost the grand sum of £2 a week. The flat had its drawbacks of course: only one power point in the whole place; we had to light the coal range before we had hot water, and the loo was not only outside, but next door. Probably the worst aspect was the rats that visited on a regular basis from the nearby Gregg's factory — they had a fondness for soap.

In order to complete his medical degree (M.B. CH.B.) as well as a Bachelor of Medical Science, Peter still had a year and a bit to go. He often had to work nights at the hospital, but I wasn't keen staying on my own in the flat, especially given the 'undesirables' who lurked about at night, and I'm not only referring to the rats! After a year we moved to a better equipped flat in Maori Hill: one that was part of the old Driver house, which had been converted from the original stables, in Drivers Road.

While Peter was fully occupied with his study, I was able to concentrate on my new job at the Home Science School. I thoroughly enjoyed lecturing in Foods, finding it challenging as well as a lot of fun. My students were keen to learn and given my own rather lacklustre experiences at the Teachers' College in Auckland, I wanted to give these young women — and they were all young women in those days — the best instruction I could.

There were usually 16 students in my class and each class lasted for three hours. We structured the course so that each time we met we covered a new topic. For an 'Egg' class, I'd demonstrate how to make an omelet then ask the students to make their own, which I'd then mark. Once this task was completed, each student was given a different egg recipe to prepare, leaving me to wander around the cooking lab helping out where necessary. Towards the end of the class, the girls brought their food up to the front and we'd taste and discuss each recipe.

I taught the same students three times a week, which meant I had to be very familiar with 48 recipes every week. Bear with me here: if you multiply 48 recipes by 30 working weeks, it adds up to 1440 recipes by the end of the year. In anyone's book, that's a lot of recipes! At that time, I had no idea that knowing intimately hundreds of recipes would stand me in good stead in the years to come.

For Food 2, I had to teach the students how to cook for a family of four. They were given a budget and instructed to create a meal using only the money allotted. I enjoyed this part of my teaching immensely and learned a great deal from these classes. I've always been budget conscious, taking as much pleasure, if not more, from preparing an economical, tasty meal as from preparing a more expensive one.

During this time, Peter was studying hard and worked very long hours. When he finished his seven years of study, we celebrated by having a brief holiday in Nelson. When we returned, he went on to complete a one-year residency at Dunedin Public Hospital in order to get his full registration.

In the early sixties, after I had been teaching for a few years, television began screening in New Zealand. At first, there was only one black and white channel, with broadcasts that lasted for just a few hours each evening. It proved to be a great novelty, capturing the attention of most New Zealanders. I well remember sitting on the bus in the mornings while on my way to work, listening to everyone discussing what had been on TV the night before.

Graham Kerr, known fondly as the 'Galloping Gourmet', was the star of the only TV cooking programme. He was a great showman, but he was a chef, not a home cook, and New Zealand women were up in arms. They complained loudly to the television network that the 'Gourmet' wasn't presenting the sort of recipes they wanted to cook for their families.

It wasn't long before the director of the former New Zealand Broadcasting Service (NZBC) paid the Home Science School a visit. He asked Miss Gray if she knew of anyone who could front a programme cooking family food on TV. She immediately suggested me!

At that time, I was also teaching cooking one night a week as part of an adult education programme. When the director of TV asked the manager of the adult classes the same question, who could front a cooking programme, she suggested me as well.

As a result, I was asked to audition for a trial programme. I was told, in no uncertain terms, that in the interests of Home Science, I needed to get down to the television studio and start cooking! Perhaps if Peter and I had at least owned a television set, I might have felt a little more confident about doing so. I'd seen very little TV and felt ill-prepared about performing in front of a camera. To make matters worse, I asked Miss Gray if she had any helpful ideas, but all she suggested was to look in the Home Science library. I searched in vain, finding only one useful fact: don't wear a patterned apron.

I decided to cook a meatloaf, one big enough to serve eight people. I was terribly nervous — I still get nervous before speaking or performing in public — but I tried to appear calm and smiled at the camera, while ostensibly showing cooks at home how to prepare the loaf. For something different, I suggested viewers embed hardboiled eggs in half the loaf before cooking. They could, I explained, serve the plain end hot with vegetables the first night, and serve the egg end cold the following night, accompanied with a salad.

The powers that be seemed happy enough with my performance, and it was decided that I was capable of cooking the type of recipes that New Zealand home cooks wanted.

Incidentally, the evening Adult Education cooking classes I taught turned out to be excellent training ground for TV. As most of my students had already put in a full day, I quickly realised that unless I was entertaining, as well as informative, they'd all fall asleep! So I had to master a few techniques for keeping their attention.

Thus began my career in television. My first programme was simply called 'Here's How: Alison Holst Cooks'. I used my own recipes, changing things a little or a lot, because that's what you do to make a recipe your own.

I wasn't teaching full-time at this stage because Kirsten, our daughter, had been born on the second of April 1964. Having a father in the delivery room wasn't usually tolerated in those days, but Peter, being well-known in the hospital, was allowed to be with me for her birth. As soon as Peter saw Kirsten, he announced, 'She's a girl!' We were thrilled with our bonny girl, beaming with proud pleasure in every photograph. I still remember the feel of her little round head and her warm, baby smell.

My mother was absolutely delighted with her first grandchild. She was more than happy to pitch in and help look after Kirsten when I needed to work, even though she didn't totally approve of working mothers. Mum

Peter relaxing with Kirsten after a hard day at the hospital, 1965.

thought Kirsten was the 'cat's pyjamas'. I'd take her up to Blacks Road, leaving the two of them sitting happily by the fire; it was a touching scene that made rushing off to work much easier. Kirsten was a smiley baby and easy in the way that happy babies are. The whole family took great delight in our beautiful little daughter.

....

NZBS set up a kitchen for me, but I had to supply everything else. Usually, I arrived at the studio by taxi, laden with the lot — everything from eggs to the pot to cook them in. If I was going to make pumpkin pie, which in those days was considered terribly exotic, I'd need at least half a dozen Pyrex dishes, all identical, with everything prepared before hand: from the bowl with flour and butter, to the rolled out pastry and cooked pumpkin, to the finished pie. I had only 20 minutes to show viewers how to cook a dish from beginning to end. It was a logistical challenge to have each and every step of a recipe visually prepared and ready to go.

From the set of 'Here's How', early seventies.

Television didn't pay very well in those days, so I had to become inventive when it came to supplying props. I put Kirsten in her pushchair and set off for Arthur Barnett's, a well-known department store. I asked if I could borrow, say six Pyrex dishes overnight. At first the shopkeepers were a bit dubious but they soon realised that if I displayed the items on TV, there'd be a rush for them the next day. You could say it was the beginning of 'product placement'. I'd take the dishes home and carefully peel off the labels so they could be replaced before everything was returned the next day.

'Here's How' aired just after the six o'clock news. Since we still didn't have a TV, Peter and I had to visit the nearby dairy if we wanted to watch the programme. Looking back on it now still makes me laugh. None of us had any experience so we learned as we went. The studio did my hair and make-up — I would never have fussed with my hair the way they did. But I had to supply all my own clothes, most of which I made myself.

After a while, I discovered trouser suits helped with the microphone cord. We'd thread it up my pant leg and attach it to my bra. It was very easy to forget it was there, causing me to become hopelessly tangled up. Sometimes I could hardly move around the kitchen. Eventually, we solved this problem by hiding a member of the floor crew beneath the kitchen bench. He'd feed out a bit of cord as I moved to and fro, but having a man at my feet took a bit of getting used to.

The programme was taped in one take, which meant I had to keep on talking until the director told me to stop. Once, while filming, a fire burst into flames at one end of the kitchen bench. I had to promptly, but grace-fully, move to the other end talking the whole time as if nothing unusual was happening! Meanwhile several of the camera crew were furiously trying to put out the flames.

No one had many cookbooks in those days, or if they did, it was either an *Edmonds* or an *Aunt Daisy*. My mother owned one or two cookbooks so worn that they no longer had covers. Most of her recipes were handwritten or clipped from newspapers or magazines. I only owned *The Basic New Zealand Cookbook*, our Home Science textbook, which had been written by Miss Gray. So I was surprised when one day a chap came into the television studio saying, we'd like you to write a cookbook for us. He was from Wellington and thought my book would do rather well.

It sounded an interesting idea, but I didn't know where to begin. 'How many pages would you expect?' I tentatively asked.

He replied, 'About a hundred and fifty pages, but don't worry, there'll be a lot of photographs.'

I went home to discuss it with Peter. We worked it out between us that I should base the book around the recipes I'd demonstrated on 'Here's How'. Fortunately I had copyright for all my recipes. It seemed a lot of pages to fill, but after much trial and error, my first book was published in 1966 by Hick Smith and Sons. And the title? *Here's How: Cooking with Alison Holst*.

It was a nicely produced, hard cover book with a colour photo at the start of each section — I still have a copy. There's a TV studio photograph of me on the cover wearing one of my Viyella dresses. There isn't the usual blurb on the back, but the book includes a variety of recipes from oyster fritters to steak and kidney pudding to marmalade. It sold rather well, too; we had to reprint at one stage, selling, in all, 15,000 copies.

It seems quite fitting that I was more than likely pregnant with Simon, our beautiful brown-eyed son, when the cover photograph was

taken—fitting as he's always been at home in the kitchen. Simon was born in November 1966, the same year Peter and I bought our first house.

The house was a lovely place situated in the 'dip' by the dairy on Highgate. It's still there, looking as good now as it did then. Peter rebuilt the fence and remembers getting a lot of barracking from Mr Scott, the timber merchant who lived across the road. Mr Scott was very critical of the timber Peter was using, but nevertheless the fence has lasted a good long time.

This is the first house Peter and I bought, at 453 Highgate in Dunedin. It was a lovely, sunny house but it became too small for us.

Kirsten at two years old, 1967.

Simon at seven months, about to be fed his special pudding by Kirsten.

As I was the first woman to cook on New Zealand television, one thing seemed to lead to another. The fishing industry suddenly discovered that if I cooked fish on TV, fish shops throughout the country sold out the next day! It wasn't long before the New Zealand Fishing Industry Board employed me. They arranged to send me to various places around New Zealand to demonstrate how to cook fish. These sessions gave me an excellent opportunity to talk to shoppers who invariably commented on 'Here's How'. Little did I know then that feedback from the public was useful market research.

My involvement with the fishing industry led me into the basement of one of Dunedin's institutions — Johnson's Fish Shop. The fishmongers taught me how to gut and fillet fish, and to identify the various types of seafood. They were eager teachers who liked to pass on their own favourite recipes.

They told me that women would come into the shop asking for a certain type of fish; the fishmongers would try and discourage them by saying, 'You don't want that. It's just shark!' But, apparently, the women replied, 'No, that's what *she* cooked on television, and that's what I want!'

The following year I wrote another cookbook, *Meals with the Family*, published again by Hick Smith and Sons. It sold even better than the first one! At least this time I knew what the publishers expected.

Our lives were very busy. Even though I managed to get a lot done during a day, Peter and I had our hands full: we had two small children, our own home and busy careers. To be truthful, I never considered my work as a career — I was too busy doing it! But I loved the variety of my life; and it was, I have to say, rather exciting.

During this time, Peter's career had also advanced. He'd moved up the hill to Wakari Hospital to complete further work in pediatrics, surgery, and radiotherapy combined with thoracic therapy. He then received a fellowship to carry out clinical duties and research at Dunedin Hospital.

In New Zealand, there is a generally recognised requirement for doctors to study overseas in order to round off a medical education, particularly so for those who want to specialise. Peter had already settled on internal medicine. He'd been awarded membership of the Royal Australasian College of Physicians, in 1967.

Probably most New Zealanders at that time were drawn to London or Edinburgh for postgraduate study, but Peter's supervisor, and subsequently good friend, Tom O'Donnell, had had experience in both the US and the UK. He recommended California saying, 'You'll have a more rewarding experience in the US.'

So, in 1968 we moved to San Francisco.

Chapter **five:**

San Francisco Opens Her Golden Gate

For us, arriving in the city we were going to live in for two years, was at once daunting, exhilarating and terrifying. The noise, the sophistication, the traffic, even the number of people in San Francisco unnerved us both. We didn't know a soul. Travelling with two small children — Kirsten was four and Simon was only 18 months old — across the Pacific left us exhausted. But after a comfortable night spent in an inexpensive, downtown hotel, we all felt much better.

The following morning, we stumbled upon a small café where we experienced our first traditional American breakfast. We watched as the cook flipped pancakes, fried bacon, sausages and eggs, and prepared hash browns with great dexterity. We had to ask what 'easy over' eggs were — fried eggs that were flipped over once the white had set around the yolk. We'd never heard of hash browns either, but they looked delicious. With our plates filled to overflowing, we traipsed to a table at the back of the café, receiving a few unfriendly looks on the way. Some customers were obviously disgruntled about children disrupting their quiet morning newspaper and coffee. The hash browns were a hit with the children who wanted me to make them as soon as we found a place to live.

While I entertained the children, Peter went apartment hunting. Our first apartment was on the corner of Carmel and Shrader streets and was within walking distance of the Moffit Hospital and the Medical Centre, Golden Gate Park, a small supermarket and a laundromat. It ticked all the boxes: a garage, two storeys, three bedrooms, a small kitchen and oil-fired central heating.

We immediately moved in, spending our first night sleeping on the carpet in the living room with just Simon's nappies to use as pillows and blankets. The central heating was most certainly turned up to high that night!

The next day we were invited to a gathering to welcome newcomers at the Medical Centre. We knocked on nearby doors until we found a babysitter for Kirsten and Simon, then set off for the party, travelling by bus. I don't remember much about the party, but I will never forget the trip home.

Half-way home, Peter and I got off the bus to buy some pillows. The thought of another night on the floor with only nappies for comfort didn't hold a lot of appeal. Clutching our pillows, we boarded another bus and sat in the back, trying to keep out of everyone's way. Then suddenly, as we were driving through Haight Ashbury, the windows of the bus started breaking. Peter and I stood up wondering whatever was happening, while everyone else hit the floor, immediately making the bus look empty. The driver, however, kept on going, driving slowly past the demonstrators who were causing the ruckus.

We thanked the bus driver as we got off. 'Oh, it was worse than this an hour ago,' he told us cheerfully. We were very pleased to get home, and paid the babysitter her fee which worked out to be four times what I would have paid in New Zealand. I quickly realised that there would be many more surprises in store for me in this interesting city. I also decided not to write about such incidents in the letters I sent home to my mother.

In the flat below us lived a couple with a little girl the same age as Kirsten. Polly and Kirsten became great playmates, while Simon quickly discovered Polly's extensive collection of toys — we'd never seen so many toys in one place before.

When Peter started work a day or so later, I took the children to a playground nearby. They excitedly ran to the assorted swings and seesaws while I sat down on the ground to watch, next to some other mothers. (The whole place was covered in woodchips.) We lived near Haight Ashbury, renowned for its hippie culture. It was the time when a lot of young women were not only wearing their hair long, but they were also wearing patterned, Indian cotton skirts that came down to their ankles. The young woman sitting beside me was watching her child play when, suddenly, she lifted her long skirt. I was startled to see a tiny baby that had been hidden under her skirt, lying fast asleep on a small shawl spread out on the wood chips. 'How old is your baby?' I asked.

'One day old,' the young woman replied.

'Why are you not in hospital?' I said.

She could see my astonishment and proceeded to tell me that she started going for regular checkups at the Medical Centre, but because she and her two-year-old often had to wait two to three hours to be seen, she stopped going. The baby's mother went on to say that, the day before, her neighbour in the flat upstairs had delivered the baby. I was left feeling very relieved that our babies had been born in New Zealand.

Gradually, our apartment became more like a home. We bought some second-hand beds and a table and chairs from St Vincent de Paul. (We liked this table so much we later sent it back to New Zealand.) A very kind neighbour offered us furniture from a deceased estate. He didn't want to be paid for anything but gave us a much needed washing machine and drier, bed linen and towels, some easy chairs, and a couch. Our landlord helped us pick up some sea-chests we'd sent ahead, but these contained mainly clothes, sleeping bags and Li-los.

Our next purchase was a car from a used-car lot in the Mission district. This vehicle gave us the freedom to go exploring on the weekends and to visit friends. Peter spent many hours in our garage with the car's instruction manual beside him, keeping the car in working order.

I used the car during the week as it suited Peter to either walk to the hospital or use San Francisco's excellent public transport system of buses, trams and cable cars. We marvelled, too, at the drivers; traffic stopped if a pedestrian stepped off the curb.

....

Peter had entered a two-year, postgraduate fellowship programme at the University of California, San Francisco campus. He was required to work at the various hospitals that were part of the University: the Moffit Hospital — one of the top ten hospitals in the US — as well as the San Francisco General Hospital in the Mission district, and at the Veterans' Hospital at Fort Miley.

In his eagerness to be accepted into the postgraduate course, Peter told the University of California that he'd received a small grant from the New Zealand government. Unfortunately, most of the New Zealand grant was quickly used up by the cost of our airfares just getting us there.

Although we were overwhelmed by everyone's generosity, for that first year in San Francisco, we were as poor as church mice. There was no extra money so we lived on $20 a week for groceries, while our friends spent about $100, but we still ate well.

Fortunately, I found an Italian green grocer only a few blocks from where we lived. He was not only friendly but extremely helpful. He sold me small eggs by the tray — I think he charged two cents per egg — and he also not only told me how to cook some of the produce on display (things I'd never seen before), he also sold me 'seconds' at much reduced prices.

This lovely man introduced me to aubergines, avocadoes and globe artichokes. Artichokes became one of our favourite foods. I'd make a mayonnaise, then simmer the artichokes in salted water until I could pull out a 'petal'. We'd dip the petals into the mayonnaise, pull out and discard the 'choke' and cut the fleshy base into quarters.

Later, when a visiting New Zealander came to dinner, I served small artichokes on our dinner plates. I forgot to tell him how to eat them and didn't notice until he had politely eaten the whole thing, petals and all! He must have thought I was a dreadful cook.

Naturally, we ate a lot of eggs. And I made all our own bread, with lots of enthusiastic help from the kids — sometimes it looked a bit grey as a result. (Bread in the US seemed very expensive when compared to what it cost in New Zealand.) I also used a lot of mince, or ground beef, as it was known there. We had everything from hamburgers to spaghetti bolognese. (I later published a mince cookbook thanks, in part, to my San Francisco days.)

While in California, I kept my involvement with the New Zealand Poultry Industry. They'd started a 'Get Cracking with Eggs' advertising campaign, and I acted as their front person. We used the catchy phrase, 'If there's an egg in the house, there's a meal in the house.' My job while overseas was to send home one egg recipe a week, which was then broadcast on radio and heard right round New Zealand. A fellow New Zealander took me to a studio where I'd record the recipes, usually three to four at a time, then send them back to New Zealand. I must have sent home over 100 egg recipes. This was a nice job for me because it brought in a bit of extra cash in addition to keeping my connection with the egg people. Sadly, I didn't keep copies of the recipes — they'd have made a good 'Egg Cookbook'.

Alison Holst gets cracking with eggs

When there's an egg in the house there's a meal in the house

For the first time in Peter's working life, he knew when he was going to have a free weekend. We took advantage of these opportunities by heading off in the car to explore the numerous regional parks in the San Francisco Bay area. Occasionally, we camped in a few of the national parks, Yosemite being our number one favourite.

These trips gave us the chance to explore the West Coast beaches, sometimes coming across otters and seals as well as the varied and unusual flowering, native plants growing in the sand hills. For us, walking in the stately redwood forests was like being in a massive, cathedral-like space, with the added bonus of the occasional bird song. We were surprised to find flowering rhododendrons, azaleas and the misty blue ceanothus (California lilac) growing wild in open spaces. Often, in early summer, we would come across blue and mauve lakes of small irises growing in meadows.

While in the forests, our eyes were always on the lookout for wild animals. The children especially loved seeing squirrels and deer at close quarters. We kept a watchful eye out, too, for bears, trying never to leave food sitting around since bears were notorious for hunting out an easy lunch. (Once, when camping at Yosemite, we woke to find that neighbouring campers had

Walking in the Californian redwood forests.

left a packet of buns in their station wagon instead of storing them in the metal box provided at each site; consequently, the vehicle was trashed by two marauding bears.) In the evenings, we'd sometimes spot raccoons prowling about or the occasional skunk — we avoided skunks at all costs. (Some years later, on the valley floor at Yosemite, we came across a mountain lion.)

Each year we took two short vacations. On a couple of occasions, we visited American friends we'd known in Dunedin: Eliza and Jim Carney, who lived in Tempe, Arizona. It took a couple of days driving to get there, so for our first trip, we chose what seemed to us the most interesting route that ran through the Mojave Desert. Even though it was December, we were astounded to see great patches of snow in the desert and after much encouragement, Peter pulled over by the side of the road so the children could play in the snow. However, the car immediately sank up to its axles in mud! Peter tried to flag down the first few passing vehicles, but they drove quickly past without a second glance. Eventually, a chap in a pickup truck stopped to pull us out but not before giving us a lecture about the dangers of stopping the car by the side of the road.

....

I first saw Julia Child's television programme 'The French Chef', while we were in San Francisco. I'd visit our neighbours in the downstairs apartment to watch her on their TV. She was so interesting and exuberant to watch. To my mind, her recipes often seemed rather complicated, but I enjoyed watching her all the same. She was such a character, a little over the top but inspiring. She had a relaxed California/West Coast style that made her charming; you couldn't help but like her. I especially liked the fact that she was taller than me. I bought her first two cookbooks, *Mastering the Art of French Cooking* and *The French Chef,* and brought them home with me to New Zealand.

We found nearly all the Americans we met to be open, friendly and helpful and made some very good friends while in San Francisco, friends that we still have today.

One day, a woman knocked on our door while Peter was at work. Dunedin neighbours had written to Doctors Dorothy and Phillip Perloff who lived in Marin County, north of the Golden Gate Bridge. Dorothy came to invite us to lunch the following weekend. As the children were playing quietly, Dorothy and I were able to talk for some time. However, as she was leaving, we discovered two little girls, completely naked, in the hall.

They had devised a game whereby Kirsten had ripped a roll of toilet paper into hundreds of bits. She then gathered up the shredded paper, ran to the top of the stairs and threw the confetti-like paper in the air. It fell below on Polly, who danced around below as if being tickled by snow. This game had kept them happy for hours. Dorothy commented that keeping the children so happily occupied, all for the price of a roll of toilet paper, was money very well spent!

Later, when we visited the Perloffs, Kirsten and Simon spent the entire time in the swimming pool. Dorothy told us that we were most welcome to swim in their pool at any time since it was seldom used. Simon, especially, loved the water. While we were in San Francisco, my friends used to borrow him so that he could show their children that it was okay to put their heads under water while in the bath. (Interestingly, he later became a very good swimmer; he and other boys from his secondary school swam across Cook Strait in a relay.)

The Carneys from Dunedin introduced us to Sherrean and Bill Rundberg who lived just south of San Francisco in San Mateo. They won the hearts of Simon and Kirsten by inviting us to their home for another American tradition, an Easter-egg hunt. Sherrean and Bill became very good friends, having since visited us in New Zealand. (We visit them regularly and have watched their children grow up.)

Sometimes, when going to visit the Rundbergs, we'd drive south along the stunningly beautiful coast road known as Highway 1. Along this route, we'd pass fields of globe artichokes and the big, golden pumpkins used mostly for Hallowe'en. Kirsten, who missed my mother, often said as she looked out over the Pacific Ocean, 'If my eyes were sharp enough, perhaps I could see Nana in Dunedin.'

We loved the warm days in San Francisco during the summer months, but the winter could be quite dreary especially when it seemed to rain day after day. Peter, probably sensing my frustrations, came home from the hospital one wintry day waving a staff circular. 'Why don't you answer this?' he suggested.

The advertisement had been written by Anne Hickey, a woman with children the same age as Kirsten and Simon. She and her husband wanted a skiing holiday and 'needed a babysitter to travel with them to Lake Tahoe for two weeks: children welcomed'. I plucked up the courage to answer the advertisement. Anne asked if she could meet us, duly arriving with her two little boys. At the end of the visit, she invited us to join them.

The three-storeyed house the Hickeys rented at Lake Tahoe.

A few days later, the seven of us packed into the Hickey's big car to drive off into the mountainous roads where the snow was piled more than ten feet high on either side. It was like driving through an endless snow canyon. Later, when we arrived at the house, the sun was shining through large windows that overlooked a bright blue lake surrounded by pine trees.

Anne, my new employer, said that in America, babysitters did not cook. She wanted me to take the children out to play in the snow for at least an hour each day, and we could then do whatever else we liked. And best of all, she cooked dinner every evening.

On the first morning, after Anne had cooked a delicious breakfast — her famous oaty pancakes, grilled bacon and maple syrup — she and Bob left to ski for the day. The children played inside very happily, amusing themselves in the large house for several hours. Eventually, after much energetic tugging and pulling up zips, I managed to get the four of them into their snowsuits, boots, mittens and hats, and off we went. They loved playing in the snow. However, after an hour or so, they'd had enough. Usually it took another hour to get everyone undressed, thawed out and to dry their clothes.

Most days, I spent hours reading while lying on a couch in the sun. In the evenings, Anne and Bob came home happy but exhausted from their day on the slopes. We'd feed and bathe the children, and while we were putting them to bed, Bob made Anne and me a cocktail. I helped while Anne cooked and we chatted about our different lives. She cooked with the casual elegance so noticeably prevalent in the sunshine state. Every night I slept like a log: my time in Lake Tahoe was more like a holiday than a job. (Anne and I subsequently became very good friends. We'd talk on the phone every few weeks and have done so for the last 40 years. To think that I might never have met her if I hadn't answered the ad.)

When Peter's summer programme started at the hospital, several other

From left: Kirsten, Buffy (the Hickey's poodle), Reed and Neil Hickey, and Simon, playing in the Hickey's garden, Marin County, California, 1970.

doctors and their families arrived from around the world to attend it, too. Alain and Laurence Junod and their six-week-old baby, Dominque, were from Geneva, Switzerland. I first met Laurence when she came to visit us, arriving with Dominique in a carry-cot. Kirsten, who was only five years old, rushed over to see the baby, but I quickly intervened, holding Kirsten back. Laurence stopped me, saying, 'Let's just see what she does.' With some trepidation, I watched while Kirsten lifted Dominique, holding her facing forward, with her arms around the small baby's tummy. She carried Dominique carefully round our living room. We later watched while Kirsten gave Dominique a warmed bottle. 'Kirsten knows exactly what she's doing,' said Laurence. 'She looks after Dominique just as well as I do, so don't worry about either of them.'

Laurence, a very charming woman, was and still is a wonderful friend. She would say, 'If you're going to do something, do it one thousand per cent, and if you're going to be sick, then go to bed properly and stay there! Your husband will manage.'

Laurence asked me to show her how to sew clothes for Dominique and to teach her how to cook American food, both of which I was more than happy to do. She taught French at night school and invited me to go, but I was too shy to attend.

One class I did attend for a couple of months was a Chinese cooking class held in San Francisco's Chinatown, the oldest and largest in North America. Chinatown was an exciting, vibrant place to visit, and unlike anywhere I'd ever been. At our class, six to eight of us sat around a large chopping block to watch while our teacher showed us how to prepare many different dishes. I was fascinated to see how she sharpened her cleaver on the unglazed rim of an upside-down plate, then chopped so fast we could hardly see what she was doing. She cooked everything quickly on a rather fierce burner while we asked lots of questions, wrote down the ingredients used, and best of all, ate everything that was cooked!

Chinese cooking was a revelation to me: I enjoyed the crunchy, brightly coloured vegetables; the way our teacher used small amounts of thinly slivered meat; the well-flavoured lightly thickened sauces. We each bought a cleaver, a stirrer, and a wok after our first class—I still have these items in my kitchen.

Peter, the children and I sometimes ate an evening meal in Chinatown for a treat. We loved the variety on offer, and meals were so inexpensive —from memory, about 50 cents a serving, including rice. We'd try something different each time, ordering from the Chinese chefs who were hurriedly cooking vast quantities of steaming dishes just inside the open door. However, you could hardly call it relaxing dining; the waiters wanted the tables emptied quickly, so we had to comply. If the children were not eating fast enough, the waiter banged our table shouting, 'Eat!'

Another couple from Toronto, Manie and Harriet Lilker, arrived for the summer programme at the hospital. They had two daughters, and Harriet and I often went together to Golden Gate Park with our children.

I called by their apartment one day before we set off to the park. It was a lovely flat with hardwood floors that extended from the kitchen through to the living room. As Harriet's two little girls ran backwards and for- wards in their little white boots, I asked Harriet if the noise disturbed Manie. (It would have driven Peter mad!)

I will never forget Harriet's reply: 'Manie says it is music to his ears. When he was a little boy during the war, he and his family were hidden in an attic, and nobody was ever allowed to make a sound.'

It was stories like Manie's and those of the many other people we met that made me realise what a sheltered life I had led in New Zealand. So many people's lives and attitudes were very different from our own. Peter was also subjected to incidents that we never expected to happen in a hospital. For example, some patients in the Mission hospital were chained to their beds with an armed policeman sitting beside them. They had usually been involved in a criminal activity. The police were to protect them from 'visitors' who may not have wanted them to talk. During our second year, the staff of the hospital were summoned by the vice chancellor. They were told, 'We're closing the campus for three days; you're all to go home.' The university was worried about student unrest. These were the turbulent years of the late sixties, after all; the country was at war and the civil rights movement was in full force.

....

At the end of our first year in San Francisco, we were offered an apart- ment that was closer to the hospital and Golden Gate Park. It was smaller but also much cheaper, so we took it. Our new flat was on one level, and it had a bigger backyard that was shared by a family upstairs who had a daughter Simon's age. It was also opposite the primary school where Kirsten would go at the start of the school year.

Once Kirsten started school, I was able to take Simon to the 'Child

Observation Centre' a couple of times a week; it cost about 50 cents a visit. For the first part of the morning, we watched our children's various activities, and for the latter part, the mothers gathered for coffee and a discussion, leaving the staff to look after the children. The leader of the mothers' group usually spoke about a particular topic, then she'd ask the group if they had anything they wanted to add. My ears nearly dropped off my head as I heard these young women discussing their often horrific problems. I didn't have any problems worth discussing, but I was very impressed by the leader's skills and the help she gave these young women.

....

Our second year in San Francisco seemed to fly by. Peter and I will never forget the unbelievable kindness of the many people we met. Around the time we were getting ourselves mentally prepared to leave, we met Dr Hartley who lived in Southern California. He had come to San Francisco to join the same programme Peter was in and wanted to discuss it with him.

Dr Hartley, in turn, invited us to Southern California to stay with him and his wife and to visit Disneyland. We thought this was a chance that our children shouldn't miss, so off we went. We didn't see much of Los Angeles itself, but we enjoyed staying at the Hartley's home near the coast. They had a large swimming pool that Simon and Kirsten thought was better than Disneyland. Simon loved the swimming pool so much that he wore the skin off his fingertips by going round and round the pool hanging on to the edge.

I was sad to leave San Francisco. It remains one of my favourite cities. Looking back, it's easy to see how living there influenced my life and my work. Most of my teachers at the Home Science School in Dunedin had studied in the US, and I was always drawn to the North American style of cooking. I liked their casual, more inventive approach. I felt very keen to take what I'd learned home to New Zealand cooks. ▪

Kirsten and Simon grew heartily sick of sitting in the back seat of the car while travelling from California to Montreal, 1970.

Camping with our tent-trailer enroute to Montreal. Kirsten and Simon still vividly remember the night the tent-trailer collapsed!

Chapter **six:**

On the Move

Most of our travel while we lived in San Francisco, apart from our excursions to Arizona, was in the state of California. We'd loved these trips so when it came time to leave, we decided to drive to our next port of call, the city of Montreal in eastern Canada —no small distance away. First, we bought a second hand tent-trailer — a pop-up tent on wheels — and set off up the West Coast to the US/Canadian border. We then found the Trans-Canada Highway and drove across the vast country of Canada to Montreal. It took us over ten days altogether.

With hindsight, the distance was probably too far for the children. Poor Kirsten and Simon were nearly beside themselves sitting in the back seat, but even so, it was a remarkable experience for all of us. We crossed the Rocky Mountains through Kicking Horse Pass, drove through the expansive emptiness of the prairies — at one point, Peter stood on the top of the car to take in the great sweep of land and the immense, blue sky —then passed through the forest and lake district of Ontario. We stayed in camping grounds set up for travellers. The car held up well (this was our second car, the first one would never have made it) covering about 600 miles a day. Peter reckoned that if we could have put the children on the roof rack, we would have!

Montreal was a splendid place. Fortunately a medical colleague of Peter's, Roy Muir, found us a place to stay when we first arrived. It was the home of another New Zealander who was about to leave Canada because his employment conditions at the University of Montreal required him to speak French. We soon moved to a small French-speaking area of the city known as the Notre-Dame-de-Grâce, or NDG.

The political situation in Montreal in 1970 was just as volatile as in San Francisco: bombs were being sent through the post; the British High Commissioner, who lived not far from us, was kidnapped; and the Canadian Government declared a State of Emergency and invoked the War Measures Act. Our children still remember his kidnapping because the CBC television network broadcast only news for the next ten days.

I remember our landlord, a French Canadian, coming to see us one night. He was clearly upset and burst into tears, claiming, 'They've murdered Pierre Laporte!' Laporte was the Deputy Premier of Quebec. On the day of Laporte's funeral, Peter was again sent home from the hospital. The army had been mobilised, there were sharp-shooters positioned on buildings, and helicopters were everywhere. It was all rather alarming.

We were impressed with the apparent bilingualism in Canada; all the road signs on the Trans-Canada Highway were in French and English; even the cereal boxes were printed in both languages. The young French-speaking women in the supermarket immediately switched to English whenever they served us. Somehow we stood out, but were never sure why.

We first discovered pizzas in Montreal. I could take the children to a restaurant where, through the window, they could watch pizza being made. They loved how the great showman confidently swirled the dough high above his head. We were soon making pizzas at home.

After four months in Montreal, we headed to London for the remainder of the year. Peter was at the postgraduate medical school at Hammersmith Hospital, next to the aptly named Wormwood Scrubs Prison. We both found London a bit disappointing after our North American experiences. It seemed dirty and archaic in comparison.

My sister, Patricia, had won a scholarship after winning the *Sydney Sun* Aria Contest and had decided to study in London. When the press called our mother about Patricia's win, she was reported to have said, 'I'm thrilled to the boots!'

We caught up with Patricia while we were in London. By her own admission, Patricia was feeling homesick and isolated at the time and was as pleased to see us as we were to see her. She had chosen a demanding and difficult path; however, opera seemed so right for her dramatic personality and big voice. We didn't know then, of course, that she was on the brink of a wonderfully successful, international singing career.

Patricia Payne: mezzo-soprano. Photo taken for the San Francisco Opera, 1977. Robert Messick

By the time we reached London we felt like seasoned travellers. However, the time had come for us to return to New Zealand, and we somewhat reluctantly turned our attention to leaving.

In early 1971, we packed up and returned to Dunedin, moving back into our house that we'd rented out while away. Although both Peter and I were convinced our home country was the best place to bring up children, we were also well aware of the disadvantages of moving back to New Zealand. Peter returned to work at Dunedin Hospital as a junior specialist, combined with a teaching position at the University of Otago Medical School.

My mother was overjoyed to have us home once again, especially to have her grandchildren back in the fold. While we had been away, my youngest sister, Clare, married Ian Ferguson; they left New Zealand soon after to see the world. I remember feeling very upset that I couldn't attend Clare's wedding; it didn't seem right.

Mum and Dad in the front garden at Blacks Road.

Having all three of her daughters living overseas had left Mum feeling bereft, but she seemed well, even though she was having trouble with her hips. On the other hand, my father's health had failed; he had developed sarcoidosis (a lung disease that makes breathing difficult) and sadly, seemed considerably older.

Once back on home ground I was pleased to find that I hadn't been completely forgotten by the food industry. Before leaving to go overseas, I'd resigned from my position at the Home Science School and was, naturally, concerned about finding work when I returned. I needn't have worried. I was asked to write another cookbook *Food Without Fuss,* which was published in 1972 by Methuen Publishers. It sold very well and was subsequently reprinted six times. I was still involved with the producer boards of the fishing and poultry industries and with a newcomer, the New Zealand pork industry, for whom I was a consultant.

Kirsten was having a little trouble settling in to school so I went along to her school to show the children how to cook a cheese fondue. Her class was delightful and sent me letters of thanks afterwards. Two I still have in my treasure box:

Room 5: Maori Hill School
Dear Mummy.
Thank you for showing us how to make a cheese fondue.
We enjoyed it. All of us have done our maths. Richard loved it. After you'd gone Richard said, I'd like some more. I said, if you go to Switzerland you will.
Your daughter, Kirsten

and another:

Dear Mrs Holst
I loved it when you came and made cheese fondue on the 9th of August.
Richard

I then agreed to work on a huge, nightmare of a book, which went on to sell over 200,000 copies. This project kept me busy for months. It was the *New Zealand Radio and Television Cookbook.* I don't think anything like it had been published before. As editor, it was my job to test the hundreds of handwritten recipes that had been sent in by people from all over the country. Most recipes needed a fair bit of correcting to make them work. Instructions like, 'heaped cups of flour' or 'a bit of this and a bit of that' wouldn't work for cooks at home. At nearly 400 pages, it proved to be quite a challenge.

My noble mother helped me test the recipes. I doubt that I would have been able to finish the project, on time, without her help. She was an intuitive and innovative cook: the perfect helpmate. In addition, Simon and his friends ate their way through dozens of cakes, biscuits and whatever else was being tested on the day. We had food coming out of our ears!

I was paid a fee for this job and was quite pleased with myself that I could afford to carpet our large hallway and living room with the proceeds. When the book came out, NZBC cleverly screened a TV series with me cooking a selection of recipes from the book. It was aired at prime time and certainly helped to ensure the book's success.

....

It was soon afterwards that my mother and father, along with Simon, were out shopping in the car. Dad started to feel unwell and they sensibly decided to go to the hospital. Mum called and asked if I could come to pick her up. Once I'd checked that Dad was all right, Simon and I drove Mum home.

In the middle of the night, Peter received a call from his colleague Tom O'Donnell. He wanted Peter to get to the hospital immediately.

Dad had died from a heart attack during the night. Although we never thought he'd make 'old bones', his death came as a shock. He was only 67. One of the hardest things I've ever done was break the news to my mother.

News of Dad's death upset Clare and Patricia terribly. They were unable to get back from the UK for his funeral. Patricia tells me that for years afterwards, she had a recurring nightmare — that of trying desperately to get back to New Zealand to be with our mother.

I immediately started work on another cookbook, *More Food Without*

Fuss, and did my best to encourage Mum to help me with that one, too. I dedicated the book to her. We all felt very sad. I bought the house next door to Mum on Blacks Road and had it made into two flats. It was less for her to look after and, as it was level, she didn't have stairs to contend with.

A cooking demonstration with my trusty frypan held at the Otago Museum auditorium in 1974. My mother was in the audience.

In 1974 Peter's colleague and friend Tom O'Donnell took up the Chair of Medicine in Wellington. He suggested that Peter apply for one of the jobs at the Wellington Clinical School of Medicine. His application was successful with the offer of a teaching position combined with clinical work.

I felt uncertain about the move at first. It seemed as if we'd only just settled since arriving back from overseas. I also didn't want to leave my mother. But, as it turned out, the move to Wellington was not only a step-up professionally for Peter, it also opened up a lot more doors for me.

We moved to Wellington in August, 1974. Kirsten was ten years old and Simon was eight.

Kirsten was the one who suffered most from the move. She'd taken a while to settle when we first came back to Dunedin, and she was also very attached to my mother. Wellington for her was very difficult at first. At one stage, I found a note from her that said, 'Dear Mum, I have run away back to Dunedin.'

We knew the way to Kirsten's heart, however. We bought a house in Karori that was at the end of a blind street. The house was near the front of the section, leaving us with a good-sized, enclosed backyard. Peter set about building a hen house, and before we knew it, we had chickens, cats, guinea pigs and a very large rabbit. Kirsten was always bringing home animals. She has a remarkably quiet, calm rapport with animals; one of our bantam hens would lay her eggs in Kirsten's hands.

Our home in Lemnos Avenue, Karori, Wellington, before it was reclad and remodelled, c. 1975.

We couldn't have chosen a friendlier street to live in. We quickly got to know all our neighbours and their children in Lemnos Avenue. One of the houses was the official home of the American Embassy, and we thoroughly enjoyed the company of the families who came to live there, usually for two or three years at a time.

Our house was within walking distance of Karori Primary School, close to shops, and near a bus stop. On sunny mornings, Peter and I would often walk, for about half an hour, from Karori, through the Botanic Gardens and down to Parliament. Peter would then take a bus from Parliament to the hospital in Newtown, and I would catch the bus back to Karori. This was always a pleasant start to the day.

During our first year in Wellington, Peter planted a vegetable garden, rebuilt an old shed to make a workshop and assembled a glass-house so we could grow lettuces and tomatoes. He also secured the fences and gates so that the backyard was animal-proof for Kirsten's growing menagerie.

To the west of our house was Johnson's Hill. Climbing to the top of the hill on a track through native bush, we got a wonderful view of the rest of Karori, the West Coast, the tip of the South Island sounds, and Wellington Harbour. At night we could hear moreporks calling from the bush. Once or twice, Peter and I walked north, along the ridge of the hills, to Mount Kaukau. From there, we walked down the hill to Khandallah, then used public transport to get home again.

....

While we were still in Dunedin, Barry Leydon from the New Zealand Meat Board came to visit me, essentially to see if I would be suitable to represent the New Zealand meat export industry overseas. I must have fit the bill because I was offered the job. Their head office was in downtown Wellington, along with various other producer boards, so suddenly, the move to Wellington started to look better to me.

Publicity photo taken at a food fair with my new book, Simply Delicious, *1975.*

Over the next decade, I travelled to a number of interesting countries to promote our quality lamb and beef. The Meat Board sent me to Honolulu, Singapore, Hong Kong, right across Canada, occasionally to the US and the UK. As I'd be away for several weeks at a time, my mother would come to Wellington to look after the children. I'd usually make at least two to three trips overseas each year.

Honolulu was my first assignment and, fortunately, Barry Leydon came with me as well as another member of the Meat Board, Gordon Dryden. They explained, in detail, the sort of things I would be expected to do and basically showed me the ropes. I quickly discovered, however, that every place I visited was different from the one before, forcing me to think on my feet.

Before leaving on these trips, I tested at least ten new beef and lamb recipes, wrote them up and arranged photography for each finished dish. These recipes would then be attractively designed and printed, so I could hand them out to the news media as I travelled.

Wherever I was sent, I would be required to demonstrate how to cook my recipes in television studios, and be interviewed by food writers from the local press and various magazines. I also cooked in supermarkets that stocked New Zealand beef and lamb, mainly to show customers 'here's how' while trying to inspire them to try our export-quality meat. Sometimes, I was asked to hold cooking demonstrations at the hotel where I was staying, usually in front of 20 to 50 local women. Afterwards, I'd invariably be taken out to dinner with the wife of a local dignitary. At the end of each day, I would gratefully unlock the door to my hotel room, ask for a wake-up call, then flop onto my bed and fall fast asleep.

I didn't get very much instruction or forewarning — usually, I'd be assigned to a public relations firm and they'd say, 'We'd like you to bring six different recipes for beef and six different recipes for lamb' (as in 'different' from last time). As soon as I'd get to the destination airport, the PR people would say, 'Here's your timetable. You start tomorrow. We need to get the ingredients ready.'

It was exhausting work, especially in Canada, where the distances between cities are considerable. I remember once leaving New York wearing sling-back shoes and arriving in Sault Ste. Marie, Ontario, to several feet of snow! Fortunately, I had the good sense to travel with a warm coat.

On this occasion, I was picked up at the airport by a PR woman and a driver, but on the way to the hotel the engine of the car blew up and caught fire. All three of us leaped out of the car, but the PR woman and I suddenly realised that we needed the carton of beef and lamb that was still sitting on the back seat. We quickly rescued the meat carton, while the driver trudged off in the snow to get help. Feeling a bit despondent, the two of us women sat on the carton, in the dark, to wait for our driver to return. At one stage a police officer came by and wanted to know who owned the burning car, but we didn't even know the driver's surname.

Eventually, I made it to the hotel. I had a seven o'clock television appearance in the morning, so I opened the carton to check the contents only to find that the meat was still frozen! Somehow I had to find a way to defrost it because I was supposed to cook it in the morning. I discovered, by padding around the room in my bare feet, that the bathroom floor was lovely and warm, so I put all the meat on the tiled floor and went to bed.

When I got up in the morning, I opened the bathroom door to find the floor was red! It was completely covered in blood. There was nothing to do but pick up the meat, put it in the sink, wipe up all the blood with the towels, put the towels in the bath to rinse and then get everything ready for the TV studio. At one stage, I opened the curtains to my room, only to see a huge iceberg floating down the St Mary's River. I couldn't help but think, 'What the hell am I doing here?'

Working for the Meat Board while overseas.

It always made me smile when people said to me, before I left on these trips, 'Have a lovely holiday!'

Something I soon learned was that ingredients from one country are not always the same as those in another. Once, while in front of a large crowd, I had an embarrassing moment that I'll never forget. I was demonstrating how to make a marinade for a lamb dish. One of the ingredients I needed was onion pulp. To make this, I had to halve an unpeeled onion crosswise, then scrape the cut surface with a teaspoon to produce a few teaspoons of onion pulp. All went well until I started to scrape the red onion that I had been given. The pulp was so strong that the tears poured down my face for several minutes! My helpers had to rush off to get me a pile of tissues. At least nobody laughed.

Travelling to different countries, of course, opened me up to endless new and interesting culinary ideas. I loved to find out what people were eating in other places, and bring new combinations of flavours home to introduce them to New Zealand cooks. I wanted to encourage cooks at home to try something a little different, but I was careful not to put them off with expensive and difficult-to-find ingredients, nor use elaborate, complicated cooking methods. I spent hours experimenting and adapting recipes using our own local, everyday ingredients. However, all the recipes had to pass the family-test, otherwise they wouldn't make it into my repertoire nor into a cookbook.

While overseas I enjoyed meeting the women who attended my demonstrations and the shoppers who stopped to chat in the supermarkets. Invariably, we'd swap recipes and exchange ideas. My kitchen skills were broadening with every overseas visit. I had to be mindful to use ingredients

Judging recipes for a lamb cooking competition with Glen Rowling in 1974. Glen and I went shopping in Arthur Barnett's department store afterwards. Glen tried on some clothes and the clerks kept saying, 'You look nice in that dear,' not realising she was the Prime Minister's wife. I didn't have the heart to tell them.

that my audience already used and liked. Soy sauce, ginger, garlic, and sesame were familiar to people in Asian countries, whereas many North Americans would not have these items in their kitchen cupboards.

On a visit to Singapore, a charming woman who lived on a plantation some distance away invited me to join her for dinner in a nearby hotel. At dinner, she wore a beautiful silk sari that draped perfectly, making her look stately and graceful. I told her I liked walking and she warned me to watch out for snakes while on the paths in forested areas. Making polite conversation, I asked her if there were problems with other animals on her property — I was thinking along the lines of pests, like rabbits. When she replied, 'Yes, tigers and elephants,' I almost fell off my chair!

On another trip to Singapore, I was asked by one of the men from the advertising agency I was working with if I would like to join him on Sunday morning to visit the Sultan of Johor Bahru. (I was so green, I thought we were off to see a race horse!) I agreed to go and we drove over a causeway to southern Malaysia, then through lush countryside for some time. I admired the archway of light-green bamboo that grew at least five metres high by the sides of the road.

Eventually we reached the Sultan's palace. We were greeted by about ten elegant silver-grey cars, each with a driver standing beside it. One of these cars took us on a grand tour; at one point, we stopped at a local hospital. Upstairs, the rooms were lavishly decorated: these rooms were where the Sultan and his family received their medical treatment. Downstairs consisted of one large ward, complete with mud floors and rows of beds: this was where the local people were looked after. It had been an interesting day but I was pleased to get back to my hotel.

If I had some free time while in Singapore, I liked to go out, just before the sun rose, to look at the various street markets. I could often buy toys or clothes for Kirsten and Simon, of a variety I'd never see at home. But I was never good at bargaining.

Only once did I buy something to eat at one of the early morning markets. I think it was some type of fish cooked in an interesting way. That night, I woke soon after going to bed, vomiting and feeling miserable. When I explained the situation the next morning, I was taken to a Chinese herbalist who listened to my colleague, mixed several powders, wrapped them in a square of rice paper, and gave them to me. I was rather doubtful about this package but felt so awful that I would have tried anything. I swallowed the mixture, and sure enough, in half an hour I was back to normal.

After this episode, I decided that I would be better off sticking with the local specialties such as Lamb Satay, in my hotel.

....

Meanwhile back at home in Karori, life became increasingly busy. I was writing books, working on radio, writing columns and planning another television series. ▪

Peter and I visiting Blacks Road in 1975. This photo was taken by my friend Martha Morseth.

A cooking demonstration for the Meat Producers Board at Mt Albert War Memorial Hall, Auckland, 1975.

Chapter **seven:**

Lemnos Avenue

I was always pleased to arrive back to Lemnos Avenue after my many trips away. It had become the hub of our lives. The lifestyle that Wellington offered suited us, and the whole family enjoyed the garden and our growing collection of feathered and four-legged friends.

With an ever increasing workload and a young family, I started to get up at 5 a.m. just to fit everything in. It soon became a firmly ingrained habit that persists even today. I set up a home office and started to write a weekly column for Independent Newspapers Ltd (INL), which in those days included Wellington and the Central North Island newspapers. My column was called 'Alison Holst's Kitchen Diary' and was eventually published throughout New Zealand. I wrote three more cookbooks for Hicks Smith and continued my consultancy work for the various producer boards I was involved with. It seemed my endorsement helped them promote their products. They also sponsored many of the cooking demonstrations I was doing throughout the country.

Talking to school children about the food of different cultures in Wellington, c. 1975.

My newspaper column was fun to do; I'd write a chatty bit first about what I was doing in the kitchen and then follow with a recipe. My kitchen habits followed a familiar pattern. In the summer we'd picnic, barbecue and relax with easy meals; harvest time would follow, with bottling, pickling and jam-making; and when the weather cooled, I'd be baking, making soups and puddings. Then suddenly it would be spring and we'd be eating asparagus and salads and looking at Christmas once again.

The column was also a great way to introduce readers to some of my more 'unusual' dishes, which had been inspired by overseas travel. In the late seventies many home cooks were still mainly using a British style of cooking, much the same as their mothers and their grandmothers had. When I first introduced stir-fry cabbage on television it caused quite a stir in itself. I remember people stopping me in the street to tell me how surprised they were that my 'crunchy cabbage' was quite wonderful.

At the end of each year my columns were collected and published as *Alison Holst's Kitchen Diaries*. At first, they were just little books; I have a copy of one that has $3.00 printed on the cover. They didn't include colour photography, but the great joy for me was that my sister Clare illustrated each page with her delightful drawings. I'd usually travel to the UK at least once a year and arranged things so I could spend a week or two with Clare. We worked on these books together. (There were twelve books in all.)

Clare had wanted to study fine arts when she finished high school, but as that required moving to Christchurch and an expense our parents couldn't afford, she too went to the Home Science School in Dunedin. At one stage, she was in my class while I was teaching there.

Clarabella, as my father called her, has her own individual style and flair, and embraces life with enthusiasm, in a similar way to our mother. In the early eighties she was working for publishers in London along with making a name for herself by working with some of the top European cooks and chefs of the day. She'd immersed herself in European cuisine, especially French and Italian, and was building an exciting career as a food stylist in a highly competitive environment.

....

With my increased involvement in the media, and the publication of my books, I was becoming more and more visible in the public arena. As a result, many companies sent me their products, free of charge, to trial. Salesmen would knock on my door, at all hours of the day, dropping off everything from packets of soup to various new electrical appliances. The thinking behind this 'generosity' was, supposedly, that if I liked their products, I might use them on television or write about them in my columns.

Everyone in the early eighties was embracing the new appliances and was keen to try them out. We were constantly being told that these new devices would make our lives much easier. I could see instantly how a food processor could certainly be used in the kitchen to good effect. I set about gathering all the information available, most of which was from American or English books and magazines, and enthusiastically tri-alled the various food processors that had been sent to me. Consistently, I found that the little booklets that were given with these appliances were confusing and unhelpful.

I loved testing and re-testing and experimenting in the kitchen. Suddenly, with a food processor, pastry became a no-mess exercise. I enthused about my food processor in one of my columns and this must have caught INL's attention because, subsequently, they invited me to write a book about food processors for New Zealand cooks. It was an inexpensive little book but it turned out to be incredibly popular.

A similar thing happened when I started experimenting with a micro-wave oven. The feedback I was getting from most home cooks confirmed that they were struggling with their new microwaves. So, I set out to write an instructive book that would assist New Zealand cooks with these marvellous time-savers. The book was a runaway bestseller, and although it's been revised many times since, my microwave book is still in print.

....

It didn't take long before the demands on my working life became so overwhelming that I could no longer manage on my own. In 1984, I decided to advertise for an assistant, but just before doing so, I gave a talk at an alumni dinner. A former student, Jane Ritchie, came up to speak to me afterwards. She reminded me that I'd taught her at the Home Science School in Dunedin. She was in Clare's year and, fortuitously, she was looking for part-time work. I offered her a job. In Jane, I found my saviour.

When Jane was in my class, I was hugely pregnant with Kirsten and, evidently, very short of breath. Jane was so alarmed by my condition — she'd been sequestered at boarding school prior to attending university, so

On the set with 'Alison Holst Cooks' in Christchurch, seventies.

wasn't at all accustomed to being around pregnant women — she decided there and then never to have children. However, she obviously overcame her aversion. By the time I met Jane again, she was married with a family of three.

Jane made my life so much easier. She was efficient, capable and firm. She was better at saying 'no' than I was. In truth, I couldn't have managed without Jane.

When Jane arrived at Lemnos Ave, I was about to start working on a new television series, 'Alison Holst Cooks', as well as a book of the same name. To put it bluntly, Jane landed in the deep end. We had our work cut out for us. All the filming for the television series was done in Christchurch, which entailed enormous organisation on our part. We had no idea what the studio would be like, but in my experience, TV usually provided the bare minimum. In other words, we had to prepare for a primitive workspace.

Our Lemnos Ave house was completely taken over by things culinary. The living room was a mass of stoves, appliances and various props to use in photographs. At one stage, I hired a housekeeper, Pam, but the poor woman never knew where to start.

The main thrust of the new television series was to encourage home cooks to use food produced in New Zealand — some of the best food in the world. While I needed to be mindful of their busy lives, I also wanted to inspire viewers to try something a bit different, to learn how to intensify flavours and produce tasty, healthy meals. I wanted my recipes to reflect the variety of produce so easily available.

I was required to write the script for each programme, showing step-by-step plans for every recipe, and send these in advance to the director, Brian Allpress. Jane organised everything we needed for our trip to Christchurch. We carefully worked out the visual steps of each recipe, ensuring that every bowl and utensil needed for filming was on our list. All the big items were sent down by truck: a stove, appliances, pots and pans, the lot. We then packed several suitcases with everything but the kitchen sink — in those days you were allowed more than one bag on planes — and off we'd go. Once there, Jane was sent off in search of red peppers and fresh herbs, the fish we were going to cook, and perhaps a utensil we'd left behind.

Each day, I started preparing food as soon as we arrived: our preparation area was as anticipated — minimal: we were given a trestle table. Jane arrived at the studio a bit later than I did, loaded with bags of food and, suddenly, with a great flurry of activity, we both tried to get everything ready for the camera. This not only included finished dishes but each and every step along the way. After all, you couldn't spend five minutes beating eggs on a 15 minute TV programme.

Using my scripts, I'd run through a rehearsal of sorts with the director. We'd break the recipe into tight sequences while I practised what I planned to say. We took notes: there needed to be a master plan and reminders for me. I thought it was useful to say things in addition to what the audience was seeing, not just reiterate the obvious. In other words, tell viewers why things are done in a certain way. We'd work out the choreography for the shoot; where the lights and camera would be; where I'd stand, etcetera; then we'd tidy up the set. I'd go off to see that my wardrobe was pressed — I still supplied my own clothes — get my hair and make-up done and then arrive back in the studio, ready to look relaxed in front of the camera. We filmed for three days.

They were long days. We'd film in the mornings and again in the afternoons. Jane acted as my sous chef and right-hand woman, working beside me, anticipating in advance everything that was to happen. The whole performance was mentally challenging, stressful and a great deal of fun. We'd banter with the crew, which helped relieve my nervousness. Once filming started, no one could make a sound because the programme was filmed in one take. I remember during one shoot, Jane realised that a sieve hadn't been included with the props on the kitchen bench. She signalled to the cameraman that he needed to quickly allow her time to sneak it into the frame. Although I found this activity distracting for a second, all went smoothly and no one was the wiser.

After three days, we packed up and took everything back to Wellington. We filmed 13 programmes for the first series.

We were also putting a cookbook together, based on the television programmes. A year or two earlier, I'd met Cliff Josephs, the new sales director at Beckett Sterling, a New Zealand publishing company on the lookout for popular Kiwi authors. Cliff had his sights set on me.

Clifford Josephs

We met for breakfast in Wellington and quickly established an easy rapport. I could see Cliff was enthusiastic about my work and wanted to take me, as he put it, 'to new levels'. Beckett Sterling offered to publish *Alison Holst Cooks* in full colour, complete with step-by-step photographs. It was the first time I was able to show readers exactly what my recipes should look like.

Becket Sterling sent the man who was to orchestrate the photography for the book, Sal Criscillo, to my home. Sal was a big, Italian chap with a personality to match his size. He was a wonderful character and had mounds of creative flair and a good eye. Colour photography was new territory for me and I wanted to learn everything I could.

Sal usually arrived towing a trailer that carried all his stuff. He had an assistant, Kathy Heath, who looked after the props. Kathy carted in boxes of beautiful bowls, simple plates and platters, as well as kitchen items that would eventually add a casual richness to the photographs. Boxes and crates not only crowded the living room and my study but were lined up and down the hallway. It's a wonder there wasn't a family mutiny, but fortunately for me, the Holst household accommodated the clutter and added activity. To Peter, Kirsten and Simon, it was business as usual.

By this time, I had collected quite a few articles of paraphernalia from antique shops to use as props; our neighbours even got in on the act. Every few days one of them would drop by with a yellow dish 'that was my mother's' or a blue patterned cloth 'picked up while we were in France'. One neighbour was so pleased to have her treasures photographed that she invited Kathy for morning and afternoon teas.

On a typical photo shoot day, Jane and I would start cooking at 7 a.m. Jane did most of the messages, dashing about Karori, picking up all the items we needed for the day. Before long, she knew all the shopkeepers: the butcher at Marsden Village Meats; Mr Chong, the green grocer, who had absolutely everything we needed and if he didn't have it, he'd get it; Mr Watt's hardware store. We used the Karori supermarkets and the Apex Four Square run by Noel and Isabelle. We found the finest fishmonger was in Courtenay Place. Jane soon worked out where to get the best bread and where she could rely on finding that little something we urgently needed back at Lemnos Avenue. She was in and out of the house all day.

....

Usually Sal and Kathy arrived about 11 a.m. ready to start work. By this time, we'd have our cooking at the almost ready stage: everything was either baking, boiling or partly done. I liked to do the finishing touches on the dishes myself before they were photographed; I'd be in the kitchen surrounded by big, steaming pots, bowls of eggs and flour, utensils of all descriptions and garnishes everywhere, sometimes even in my hair.

Sal knew exactly what he wanted. He'd make some space for himself in amongst the clutter and set to work. The light had to be right, and the trifle had to be in a glass dish so we could see the fresh fruit, and the photo had to be taken while the custard for the trifle was being poured into the beautifully shaped goblet. The fish dishes needed to be perfect: fillets placed on a white plate with a bit of lemon, parsley, and a red napkin casually setting off the whole with a little silverware off to the side. Nothing was allowed to overpower the main event: the food itself.

As a team, we collaborated and co-operated like clockwork; it was often quite late before we'd call it a day. Jane was always a companionable presence in the kitchen. I made sure that I greeted the children when they came in from school, and as soon as Peter came home from the hospital, we'd have a drink together and a catch up. Then I was back in the kitchen. The family feasted well on the finished dishes.

The original screening of 'Alison Holst Cooks' was aired on Sunday afternoon, which turned out to be a disaster for us. No one watched it. But dear Cliffy, as I fondly called him, persuaded someone in TVNZ to move the programme to the Friday night slot at 7:30 p.m. and, suddenly, it was an instant success. Our book went from sales of 10,000 copies to selling over 100,000 before the year was out.

To mark this achievement, my publisher, Beckett Sterling, along with Cliff and all the participants involved, presented me with a specially bound copy of the book at a party held at Il Casino, a popular restaurant in downtown Wellington. It was a pleasing moment, one I still cherish.

Unfortunately, I couldn't indulge in the champagne on offer because, the next day, I was due for surgery.

....

I first met Sharon Crosbie in 1978 when she interviewed me for radio on *All Things Considered*, a programme that covered politics and lifestyle. A few years later, we met up again in the UK. Sharon was staying in a B&B in London. I invited her round to Clare's apartment for dinner. At that time I had been helping Clare prepare food for a Robert Carrier television programme. Clare and I made Sharon a chocolate tart and that simple act seemed to warm her heart.

Sharon and I decided to go to Harrods together the following day. We had great fun looking at all the clothes and luxury items, as well as being 'gobsmacked' (Sharon's word) by the expense of everything. At one point Sharon held up a belt that cost £500. We New Zealanders had great difficulty taking such prices seriously. My jaw dropped when we witnessed a woman purchasing a £5000 gown with cash.

I wanted to go to Harrods Food Hall to buy one of their famous game pies. In true Kiwi style, Sharon and I found a place to sit down, covering our laps with paper napkins. I then placed the pie on my lap and pulled out my Swiss Army knife. We proceeded to have a picnic while watching the shoppers scurry about, laughing our heads off, having the time of our lives.

On the way home we stopped at an Indian restaurant that had been highly recommended to us. It was near Albert Hall and was decorated with palm trees similar to the nikau palms we now see surrounding the Wellington Central Library. It was all quite flash, and we ordered several dishes, asking the waiter if we'd ordered enough food. He waved his hand about and shook his head, but then proceeded to bring us course after course after course. At about dish number fifteen we pleaded, 'no more, please', but more came. It was all delicious and we ate the lot.

On the way home, we window-shopped, picking up a marzipan treat for Peter; it was in the shape of a woman's leg complete with a high-heeled shoe. That day was really the start of our very long and warm friendship.

Once back in New Zealand, Sharon invited me to be a regular guest on her morning National Radio programme. She hosted the nine to noon slot, interviewing political and social commentators throughout New Zealand and around the world. One moment she'd be interviewing Prime Minister Robert Muldoon about the price and wage freeze and the next be talking to an English correspondent in London about royalty.

She and I talked about food for nearly half an hour every Thursday. We did this for a number of years and it greatly helped that Sharon loved food and cooking, and was extremely knowledgeable. She'd never let on of course; she played the role of the no-hoper in the kitchen.

Sharon Crosbie and I in one of the radio studios, c. 1983.

Occasionally, I'd arrive at Broadcasting House on the Terrace, straight from a photo shoot, covered in flour, and I wouldn't have a clue what Sharon had told listeners to expect. One day it would be 'Today, Alison Holst will tell us how to cook kapok pillows.' Another time, she promised I'd tell listeners what to do with their old wooden spoons and empty egg cartons.

But usually we'd discuss how to make the most of what was in season or, because we had the time, we could cover how to bake bread or can peaches.

Sharon could be quite mischievous while we were live on air. Sometimes, she'd abandon the studio, leaving me talking on my own with no idea when she'd return. Once, she crawled under the desk only to pop up with black felt whiskers drawn on her face. I had to keep talking with a straight face while Sharon pulled some outrageous, but nonetheless creative antics, all designed to put me off my stride.

Listeners apparently enjoyed our sessions on air. It was a testament to Sharon's abilities as a public broadcaster that we were able to discuss everything from Christmas cakes to how to serve the perfectly cooked steak, and never repeat a subject or miss a cue in all the years we were on air. ▦

Changing styles!

1966

From left: Margaret Tait with Jesus turkey, Kirsten holding Quack and Simon with Biddy the bantam hen, at Lemnos Avenue, Karori, Wellington.

Chapter **eight:**

Four-legged and Feathered Friends

Peter and I have always believed that it is important to teach children to be kind to animals and for them to have animals to love and care for. We have always enjoyed the various animals and birds in our lives.

From the time Kirsten could walk confidently, she paraded around my parents' garden at Blacks Road with Sherry Pup, our family dog, for hours at a time, holding her leash. When Kirsten got tired and sat down, Sherry Pup would lie down beside her, with her head on Kirsten's knee. Sadly Sherry Pup died quietly of old age, not long before we returned from California.

While we lived in San Francisco, we couldn't have animals, since we were renting and no pets were allowed. We decided that a few giant tadpoles the children had caught themselves and a fresh-water crayfish wouldn't be breaking the rules. In time, we let our little creatures loose again, in Golden Gate Park, and watched them swim and scuttle away.

When we moved to Wellington, gradually, and mainly due to Kirsten, our backyard filled up with animals and birds. I've already mentioned the henhouse and run that Peter built and Kirsten's special bond with one of our bantam hens. We also had a large cage with a number of very friendly, talkative budgies whose company we greatly enjoyed. Peter built a number of nesting boxes for the females in order to stop wars from breaking out amongst the pairs. (Simon keeps budgies to this day and I love hearing their familiar chattering in the background when we talk on the phone or when I visit.)

Then we got Demelsa, a very large, white rabbit, who belonged to one of Peter's colleagues at the hospital. Demelsa had had the run of her owner's flat, but kept eating through various electrical wires, so, eventually, she was put in a carton and brought home to us. Demelsa lived happily in the henhouse with the bantams. Not long after, a guinea pig that we had been given joined the menagerie in the henhouse. It made us laugh to see the bantams wandering round their run, with Demelsa lying comfortably on her side, sunbathing, while the guinea pig cuddled up close to Demelsa's tummy. The big rabbit's paws were usually gently placed around the little guinea pig.

Eventually, Kirsten decided that our guinea pig was lonely so we decided another female guinea would probably be good company for her. Fortunately, the two got on well together. We had read an interesting article about guinea pigs — it suggested using a fence of green mesh (the kind that is sometimes put in spouting) around the hutch door to give the guinea pigs a run. Every few days the fence was to be made longer and cover a bigger area giving the animals more and more space to run around and naturally more grass to eat. Ultimately, the fence was to be removed, leaving the guinea pigs within the invisible fence line. This idea worked very well.

Then Kirsten asked if we could have 'just one batch of baby guinea

Simon and Kirsten with Nana Payne (my mother) and the teddy bears she made for them.

pigs'. A male guinea pig was imported for a day or two and sure enough, it soon became obvious that one of our two female guinea pigs was pregnant. Her tummy got bigger and bigger, until her little legs could hardly touch the ground. She looked like a big, furry bulge. One morning, when we didn't see the guinea pigs outside their hutch, we looked inside to find the two sitting close together. (Aunty guinea pig had been very considerate and attentive throughout Mother guinea pig's pregnancy.) An hour or two later, we discovered both the females licking several baby guinea pigs. We didn't want to interfere because the young, who looked just like miniature adult animals, were absolutely fine and lively. A few days later, the females took the babies outside their cage to run around on the grass, and we saw, to our surprise, that the young would run to either female to be fed.

A little while later, we met a biologist who lived on a farmlet in the Ohariu Valley, which is between Karori and the west coast. Helen lived in a house surrounded by several green paddocks. There was a stream running through the property that filled a pond — a perfect catchment for the various ducks and geese that visited from time to time. Helen regularly invited us to come and see the latest additions to her collection of farm animals.

When we were first introduced to Helen's donkey, the donkey was pregnant. When the baby donkey was born, the mother apparently dropped it in the paddock, walked away and sadly would have absolutely nothing to do with it. We went to visit the donkey foal several times during the weeks after its birth. I don't think I have ever seen such a beautiful little animal. Its coat was like velvet; it had huge, extra-soft ears and big eyes with long, long eyelashes. This little foal happily drank milk from a bottle.

While it was very young, the foal lived in the kitchen, alongside a sheepdog that had recently given birth to at least half a dozen puppies. Four large, solid planks had been nailed together to make a fence around the kitchen table legs, so the little pups could be contained. This system worked remarkably well; the mother would lie peacefully on her side while the puppies crawled all over her. The young donkey stood nearby.

This beautiful little creature certainly had no idea how to fold up its legs and lie down: it would drink all the milk from the bottle, then fall asleep standing up, only to fall sideways on to the floor, but continue to sleep on.

One day, Helen gave us a duckling to take home. Its mother had abandoned it and like all ducklings, it was beautiful. Kirsten and Simon used to take Quack into the bath with them and dry him afterwards with the blow-drier. Quack lived in a low-sided cardboard box in my study for a little while, but then he decided that it was much nicer to sit on my feet while I worked at my desk. We realised, as Quack got bigger and bigger, that he was a Muscovy duck. They get very large indeed.

I soon discovered that it wasn't possible to house-train a duck. I experimented; first I cut and hemmed a square of blue and white gingham, then placed a couple of paper towels on top. I found a large safety pin, sat Quack on my knee, positioned the nappy between his legs, brought the four corners up so they met at the tail end of his back and put the safety pin in place. At first, I thought Quack might sulk, but he didn't care at all, and ran around the house quite happily with his nappy in place, then sat down on my feet again.

These were the days when a number of salesmen would come to the door. Sometimes they were arriving with a later model of some kitchen appliance, or they wanted me to try out some new product. When the front door bell rang, I'd try to slip my feet from under Quack, and leave him half-asleep in my study. When he heard my voice, however, he would rush out of the study and up the hall to the front door. I always ignored him. He'd stand beside me with his neck extended, hissing at the visitor. The astonished salesmen would keep glancing at Quack, but I wouldn't introduce them. The men usually left with rather puzzled expressions.

Not long after this, somebody gave us a turkey egg. We thought that it would be interesting to see if we could hatch this egg. Peter worked out how to set up an incubator in his workshop. He kept the egg warm in a lined box, complete with a light bulb and a thermometer. The day before Christmas, Simon came in from the workshop and told us that the egg was 'peeping'. We all went out to look at the egg, and sure enough, little noises were coming from the egg. Peter bored a small hole through the shell, so the chick could get some air. Nothing happened. The next day being Christmas Day, we all went off to church. When we got home, we went out to the shed and found that the egg had hatched! Our latest baby was beautiful—none of us had ever seen a turkey chick before. He had a long neck, and instead of being plain yellow in colour, he was flecked with black. What would we call him? It seemed obvious to the children — he was named Jesus. He thrived, grew quickly and joined the other various birds and animals that ran loose during the day, round the garden.

Kirsten sometimes travelled north on the bus to visit Peter's parents. They lived on a couple of acres in Bainesse, near Levin. She often travelled with her white mice nestled comfortably in her pockets. It wasn't all that comfortable though, for the poor, unsuspecting person who sat next to her on the bus, especially when they saw a white mouse jump out of her pocket. Her grandparents would meet the bus and take Kirsten back to their place. There was a dairy farm next door where Kirsten loved to visit. She'd help with the milking and herding the cows back out to their paddocks. One day the farmer offered to give Kirsten a new-born calf, one that she desperately wanted. I had to draw the line saying that a small, suburban backyard was no place for a cow!

We were becoming a bit concerned because Quack didn't have anywhere to swim. Early one Sunday morning, we visited the Katherine Mansfield

Memorial Park, where there was a little stream and a pond lined with concrete. We put Quack in the water to swim, but were surprised when he sank. We decided that, if we walked alongside him in the water, single file, he might paddle along behind us. We did this

Peter with his father, Erik, his mother, Cassie, Simon and Kirsten.

but he wouldn't come into the water. We lifted him in, and he sank again. We gave up and took Quack home.

Not long after, I was interviewing a young woman for a job. She looked out of the window and saw Quack. 'Oh', she said, 'my aunt lives in a flat overlooking the Katherine Mansfield Park. The other day, she saw a family carrying a big bird just like yours to the pool there. They all walked along, single file, in the water. My aunt thought it was a very strange performance.'

'Really,' I said. 'Fancy that!'

Quack, by this time, had grown very large. He eventually joined the other animals in the back garden. One Saturday, Kirsten went out to feed all her animals, and found that Quack was missing. We hunted high and low, without results. Kirsten decided to ring a radio station, and sure enough someone rang us. 'We've got a bloody great goose sitting on our roof,' said the caller. We drove to his address, and sure enough, there was Quack. He had obviously got lost and was delighted to be brought home.

Quack was the most sociable of all the birds in the garden at this time. If I was kneeling down, gardening or trimming edges, he would stand beside me 'whuffling' my hair. However, Quack took too much interest in the young turkey. One day he grabbed it by the neck, much too enthusiastically, and sadly, killed it.

We decided, after this, that Quack should go back to Helen's farmlet. A month or so later, the children and I drove back to visit the donkey and the other animals. We stopped the car some distance from the house and I said something to the children as I opened the car door to let them out. Suddenly, out of the blue, Quack landed at our feet. He had heard our voices and obviously wanted to come home with us. All's well that ends well, however. Quack and a young female Muscovy duck were sent to a farm many miles away, and we were later told that the two of them lived happily ever after.

Remembering our teen years

My parents bought land at Manakau, a small settlement not far from Levin, after we moved to Wellington. I think it was about 1976. It was Dad's garden plot (and it still is). He planted a great variety of trees that have grown to tremendous heights. He also planted citrus trees and established an enormous vegetable garden. When we were kids, they took us up there on Sundays to garden! First, they built a garage and later, when I was away at university, Mum and Dad had a Lockwood home built on the property.

We had great fun at Manakau, apart from the gardening, and often took our friends with us. At one stage I went with a group from school to pick fruit as a summer job. While at Manakau, we often went to Waikawa Beach and loved to spend our time in the sea digging for tuatuas and trying to drag net for fish. Apart from crabs we rarely caught anything. Simon and his best friend at high school, Adam Perrott, were great swimmers and could show their prowess by dealing with the deep end of the net.

My brother and Adam were into long distance swimming and they trained together. Because of all their swimming, they were always hungry and ate HUGE quantities of food. The two boys were surprisingly interested in food and not only because of their massive appetites. They could speak intelligently about the intensity of flavours and were inquisitive about ingredients, knowing full well how to savour a fine dish. These were wonderful traits to have in a house like ours. Mum was always trying out new dishes and these two could give an impressive opinion on three different versions of a particular dish. As an after school snack, they could consume several family dinners!

I remember Simon, at one point, saying to Adam, that there was no point getting to like anything too much as it was likely to be just a 'phase'. Adam's family was a bit unusual for those days: he had one brother and two sisters, and the boys learned to cook, sew and knit right along with the girls. Adam's brother, Jeremy, who lived with us a bit later in Palmerston North, phoned me one day while I was on call, wanting to know which jar in the pantry held the self-raising flour.

Kirsten, July, 2011

Chapter **nine:**

Have Frypan, Will Travel

During the eighties and nineties, I carried out many cooking demonstrations in town halls and school auditoriums throughout New Zealand. No place was too big or too small. One week I'd drive north to a small town in the middle of the Manawatu and the next, catch a plane and fly to a remote town in the South. There were two reasons for my travel: first, I wanted to teach young mothers to cook, especially when they were just starting out. I set out to show them how to cook meals they could afford and ones that I knew they would enjoy cooking for their families. The second reason was that through these events — I usually did about 40 to 50 a year — we raised millions of dollars for Plunket, kindergartens and schools. I was told that because people had seen me on television, they were curious and came to my demonstrations to see what I was really like.

We had very good audience numbers in most places we visited. Usually the local Lions Clubs or community groups organised the events. They would sort out the hall and advertise the fact that I was coming. Of all the events, I think the largest was held in Invercargill where I appeared in the town hall. Jane organised all the bookings and planned my travel; we were sometimes booked a year in advance. If possible, I'd fly to a destination city for a 'dem', then rent a car and hold cooking demonstrations in one or two nearby small towns. We had a list of my requirements and Jane sent it well in advance to the organisers. I needed electric outlets, tables the right height, good lighting, a microphone (although my teacher's voice carried quite well), wooden chopping blocks, a microwave oven, a food processor, buckets, paper towels and so on. My sponsors supplied most of the ingredients and, at times, cooking equipment.

My special canvas bag went with me whenever I travelled; it lay flat and was made up with half-pockets which I filled with the tools of my trade: measuring spoons and cups, various sharp knives and scissors, wooden spoons and spatulas, whisks and the like. This bag rolled into a convenient, albeit lumpy, cylinder shape that secured with ties. This way I could see at a glance that everything I needed was packed and that my helpers who washed up had put my tools back in place. (I'd never be allowed on planes today with my very sharp knives, even if they were wrapped up in my tool-kit.)

I also travelled with an electric frypan. To my mind, it was one of the most reliable and convenient appliances available. When boarding a plane, invariably, the handle of the frypan would be sticking out of my bag. The other passengers — they were mostly men in those days — were probably thinking I'd run away from home. Many was the time when my frypan was the only cooking device I had available while demonstrating in front of several hundred people. I used to joke, 'Have frypan, will travel.'

Before a demonstration, it was vital that I arrived at the hall early enough to ensure that everything I needed was in place. I also liked to meet the organisers and tell my helpers exactly what I wanted them to do.

Once I had checked the food preparation, I preferred to be taken to my room for a quiet hour and, perhaps, have a bowl of soup.

I always asked for a long counter to be set up on the stage. To start, I'd prepare the first dish on the right hand end of the counter, then I'd move over to the left end to prepare the second dish, while two helpers not only cleared up after me, but put everything I needed for the third dish in place. This way I never had to have my back to the audience and I could move smoothly between one recipe and the next.

The whole time I was chopping and cooking, I explained how and why things were done, chatted about the way my family liked this particular dish and told people what we usually served with it. I'd complete each recipe and put it aside on a separate table so the audience could see for themselves what the finished dish looked like at the end of the evening. (I usually asked people to keep their hands firmly clasped behind their backs when they came up to have a look, so that everyone got a chance to see the finished dishes.) We always arranged to give out printed copies of the recipes I had prepared, so people in the audience had something to take away with them.

When I'd finished cooking, people could buy cookbooks, which I was happy to sign, and purchase the knives I used — every cook needs at least one good quality, sharp knife in the kitchen. (I imported Swiss knives that I thought were better value for money than knives available in local hardware stores.) I enjoyed meeting people from the audience and usually found a number of fascinating enthusiasts. Sometimes, I'd meet a keen gardener and before I knew it, he was taking down my address in order to send me some precious heritage seeds.

Many of the women who came to my demonstrations were keen cooks, and they'd tell me how they prepared roast chicken or what they did with their over-supply of green beans. My audiences were incredibly generous with their ideas; many sent me recipes of their own. These events not only kept me in touch with the grassroots, they were a source of great inspiration. I got more from these encounters than people realised. Invariably, I picked up at least one or two ideas that I couldn't wait to try out in my kitchen at Lemnos Avenue.

From a young age, Simon and Kirsten were both more than capable in the kitchen, having grown up with cooking and food preparation as a big part of their daily lives. Simon claims it was 'constantly in the background'. When they were in their teens, I taught them how to prepare an evening meal; when I was away they took turns at this, seeing it as something of a challenge. Sometimes my mother came to stay, but if I was only going to be away for one or two nights, Peter would be there in the evenings and my family were more than capable of looking after themselves.

When I was travelling overseas, my mother came and stayed with Peter and the children or occasionally occupied a house down the road while the owners were away. Later, we bought her a flat nearby where she could

Mum with her family at a wedding. From left: Mum's niece Margaret; her brother John; Mum; her sisters Kath and Nellie, and her brother Allan.

be independent, but we could never persuade her to permanently relocate to Wellington. She always preferred to eventually return to Blacks Road.

Mum suffered from arthritis in her hips, having had three hip replacements over a span of 15 years. Arthritic hips are obviously genetic in the family as both my sisters and I have had similar problems with ours. But Mum was indomitable, never letting on she was less than hale and hearty.

....

In 1985, while I was travelling for the Meat Board, I spent a week working in New York. Sharon Crosbie was there at the same time; she'd been awarded a one-year fellowship in journalism at Harvard University. When she finished her fellowship, she left Boston to work at the *New York Times* and the Council for Foreign Relations in New York.

It was lovely to be in her familiar company again, especially since travelling, as I had been, meant I was constantly coming into contact with new people. My New York hosts were overjoyed to hear I had a friend in the Big Apple and gave us tickets to see *Cats* together. They were so relieved that they didn't have to sit through it yet again, as they'd seen it once too often while hosting overseas guests. Sharon and I went along and had a ball.

I was tired of hotel food by this time and, knowing there was a market across the street from Sharon's flat—she lived on East 87th Street—I arrived at her door very early on a Saturday morning laden with armfuls of fresh vegetables. I was desperate for some greens and immediately set to work cooking up a storm in her tiny, tiny kitchen. It was an unusual breakfast feast, and I'm not sure whether to credit the vegetables or the accompanying laughter, perhaps both, but Sharon and I devoured every last scrap and felt much the better for it.

Jane's and my day-to-day working life back at Lemnos Avenue was relatively quiet but productive. Jane and I tested and re-tested recipes. To ensure that the oven temperatures I was recommending were correct, we carried out regular experiments with thermometers as a guide. Before I could honestly endorse a product or appliance, I liked to make sure it met a certain standard; we trialled these too. Besides doing the food shopping, Jane, with the help of my accountant and good friend from school days, Shirley Jones, sorted out most of my paper work and looked after my accounts. And of course, there was the never-ending cleaning up. I also needed quiet time to write, to read and to explore new ideas.

It turned out that preparation for the 'Alison Holst Cooks' TV series and the accompanying book, was only a prelude to what was to come. Cliff Josephs organised with TVNZ to produce a television series called 'Alison Holst – Cooking Class'. It was based loosely on the Delia Smith TV series that had proved popular in the UK. We were to develop three separate series, as in 'Cooking Class—One, Two and Three' with each 'class' comprising 13 episodes. Beckett Sterling was the executive producer, which meant Cliff had to find sponsors to help fund the programme, and find them he did. Beckett Sterling also commissioned me to write the three accompanying cookbooks.

Suddenly, Jane and I moved into a new gear. We worked on book one first. I planned the structure of the book, breaking it into various sections, from starters and snacks to jams and jellies, sticking mainly to the fundamentals of cooking but adding enough culinary sophistication to inspire busy, intuitive cooks. I decided to include a wide range of information: how to cook raw mussels; how to make an Indonesian sauce; how to make hummus, sprout beans, and how to make plenty of quick chicken dishes. My section on getting the best from green vegetables, started with this plea: 'Don't boil them to death!'

Once again, Sal, my book photographer, knew what he wanted; the

The crew at Avalon Studio, Wellington.

photographs of the finished dishes were beautiful, with the food remaining the star attraction. He used either a stark white background or a dramatic black to great effect. These set off the foods exquisitely. We felt a real sense of accomplishment when we finished the photography for the book.

For this series, we didn't have to travel to Christchurch to film; it was all done at Avalon, the TVNZ studios in Lower Hutt. Cliff arranged to have a beautiful kitchen built on the premises, complete with a greenhouse window, the latest appliances — including a smart cooktop stove that had a barbecue unit — and an effective bench-height fan. I took my own pots and pans, plants and pictures, my own kitchen utensils — I liked to use familiar tools — and a food processor and microwave oven. These helped me to cook efficiently and quickly — after all, I only had half an hour.

But this was the show-kitchen. The *real* kitchen, where all the preparation was carried out, was situated in the dark recesses of Avalon, a long way from the set. Jane organised all the 'prep' with some assistance from Patricia Walker, a Toshiba demonstrator. She also had someone to help wash dishes and various other fetchers and carriers on hand. We arrived at the makeshift kitchen to find a dirty sink and an old rug on the floor while having to step over ladders, empty paint cans and left-over timber from other sets—if viewers could only see behind the scenes! With workers coming and going, it wasn't the most salubrious of workstations.

Jane had a huge task ahead of her; we carefully made lists, and lists of lists to ensure all necessary items would be at the studio when we needed them. Avalon provided nothing; we had to pack absolutely everything in suitcases and cart it all out there.

Jane Ritchie and I making a last minute check before filming begins.

My scripts needed to be meticulous, with everything fitted into exact time-slots. The recipes had to be broken into simple, easy-to-follow steps and I needed to know exactly where and when to act, which camera to look at, and what I was going to say. Meanwhile, out the back, Jane had to prepare everything from a bowl of golden syrup to a cup of chopped parsley and have it delivered to my pretty kitchen right on cue.

I worked with a large crew. There were three camera men, a floor manager, Steve Gray, who made sure everything ran smoothly—he flashed cards in front of me, signalling when to start and stop, and he transferred information to and from the control room. It was an upstairs/downstairs arrangement with the producer of the series, Gordon Ell, the director, Tony Wilson, and various technical people seated above us in the control room.

I didn't become involved with the food preparation behind the scenes this time; Jane and I had already planned the whole shooting match right down to the finest of details. Instead, I focused on what would appear on screen. My wardrobe was co-ordinated by my long-time friend, Dawn Morrison, who not only designed some of my outfits but made many of them, too. She chose jewel-like colours so that I stood out from the mostly grey and white kitchen — deep, bright blues, crimson reds, emerald greens — all beautifully accented with big, bold, colourful scarves. I felt quite glamorous once Dawn had finished with me.

On days we were filming, Jane usually rose at 4 a.m. so she could get out to the studio early and start working. I arrived a bit later, noticeably distracted, thinking about the day ahead. And they were long days — we never finished until late in the evening. Thankfully, the floor crew was a lot of fun. Their jibes and jokes helped put me at ease. Someone had the bright idea of sticking coloured bows on the cameras so I could see which one I should be looking at.

As soon as we finished filming, the crew descended on the food like a flock of crows, devouring everything in sight. Many was the time Jane and I left the studio late at night, starving. After we finished one take, we found out that something had gone wrong and it had to be shot again. But the crew had eaten every last cabbage roll and we only ever made enough for one shoot. What to do? I rushed out the back, found some cabbage leaves, ran them under hot water, then proceeded to stuff them with paper towels. We placed them on the plate with the appropriate garnishes and no one was any the wiser. However, that was one dish the crew did leave for us.

We found Beckett Sterling to be very generous publishers. After we'd finished a project, whether it be photographing for a book or filming a series, they sent flowers and bubbles, and they took us to beautiful restaurants for lunch. They made us all feel special. 'Alison Holst – Cooking Class' was broadcast in 1986, with the accompanying book released at the same time.

As things were getting increasingly busy, I hired Dee Harris. She became part and parcel of our team. Dee knew about computers — something neither Jane nor I knew much about — and I came to rely on Dee a great deal. We completed 'Cooking Class Two' the following year, followed in 1988 with the third in the series. A book was released with each programme. It was a successful run and I've always been grateful to Cliff for taking me 'to new levels'.

....

Suddenly, our children seemed grown up and were talking about leaving home to follow their chosen paths. Kirsten announced that she wanted to study medicine at the University of Otago. We'd thought she wanted to be a pharmacist because at high school she had worked during the vacations at the local Karori Pharmacy. Both Peter and I thought she was choosing a very difficult row to hoe; however, we'd brought her up to make her own way in the world and we would support her no matter what she had decided to do. We always maintained that she must be able to support herself and her children, if need be, and to be in a position where she could make choices for herself and not be dependent on anyone else.

Kirsten followed in Peter's footsteps and moved to Dunedin, staying at Knox College for the first year. During her second year, she went flatting near the Gardens and became very friendly with Mark Buxton, a school friend from Karori. In the middle of her second year, Kirsten and Mark arrived at our door to tell us that Kirsten was pregnant. Naturally, tears were shed. Peter's response was similar to my own — there were worse things that could happen. He also reassured Kirsten by saying that one of the best things that had happened to him was meeting me and having children of his own.

By a strange coincidence, I had only that day washed all Simon and Kirsten's baby clothes, the garments that I had made. They were laid out carefully on Kirsten's bed. We could only but laugh at my timing.

Four generations: my daughter Kirsten holding Elizabeth Buxton, my mother, Margaret, and me, 1985.

Kirsten, in typical fashion, had already been to see the dean of the med school, who advised her to continue with her training. He suggested that she could take her baby along to classes and feed her in the projection room — according to him, it wouldn't be a problem. And continue with her studies she did. Kirsten gave birth to a beautiful little girl who they called Elizabeth. As the dean had suggested, Kirsten took her baby to classes and her fellow medical students often carried Elizabeth in her carry-cot up and down the stairs for her.

We supported them as best we could, organising to have another room built onto the house at 104 Blacks Road where my mother now lived. Mum was in the flat at the front and Kirsten, Mark and Elizabeth moved into the back. Mum was delighted at the prospect. She wasn't well enough to look after her great-granddaughter, but she loved to read to Liz, and Liz could never get enough of story time.

In Kirsten's final year at medical school, she became gravely ill. She had developed colitis, like my mother, and had to have drastic surgery. Kirsten was only just well enough to walk across the stage at her graduation ceremony held in the Dunedin Town Hall. When she received her degree, the other students cheered loudly and filled the hall with their applause. Peter and I marvelled at her strength of character.

Meanwhile, Simon chose a completely different course. At first, he got a job with the Trust Bank in Wellington, working in the heart of the city. But after three or four months, he was transferred to Johnsonville, a suburb of Wellington. Here, his colleagues were part-time, married women and as he put it, 'Johnsonville was hardly the hub of the universe at lunch time.' He decided to go to the University of Victoria for a year, then moved to Christchurch where he completed a science degree at Canterbury University.

The house at 104 Blacks Road, next door to my parents' house, which I bought and turned into two flats. My mother lived in the front flat and Kirsten, Mark and Elizabeth lived in the back.

Simon and my mother Margaret were with me at Government House when I received a Q.S.M. 1985.

Family photo taken at Lemnos Avenue, Karori. From top left, Mark, Kirsten, Elizabeth, Simon, me and Peter.

Chapter **ten:**

From Kitchen to Pantry

The state of our Lemnos Avenue home remained chaotic. My kitchen bulged with culinary gadgets, bottles of this and jars of that, appliances of all descriptions, various casserole dishes and lovely bowls of every colour. The study was crammed with boxes and piles of papers and magazines. It seemed every time we took on a new project, more stuff would arrive, filling the spaces we'd just cleared. Jane did her best to keep a semblance of order, but it must have seemed like a thankless task.

When I look back now I wonder how my family managed, but I hardly noticed the clutter. The kitchen was my laboratory, the hallway and lounge was the storeroom and the study was the engine room that drove everything. I was up to my eyeballs in fulfilling work and I loved it.

Beckett Sterling Publishers had an instinct that a big microwave oven cookbook would be 'the next best thing'. I tended to agree. The now well-practised team of Jane, Dee Harris and I started work immediately on the book: writing, researching, testing, rewriting, re-testing. Who knows how many microwave ovens we put to the test. I had to think long and hard about what was important to a home cook when using a microwave and how best to put these time-savers to work.

As soon as Sal Criscillo and Kathy Heath became involved, we watched this project grow, and grow some more, into something quite splendid. *The New Microwave Cookbook* was an enormous undertaking. We wanted it to be the definitive book on microwave cookery in New Zealand. Not only were the recipes extensive, we included everything from what sort of dishes to use to how to defrost frozen goods, as well as instructions for improving the appearance of food and many pages of microwave 'tips'.

The photographs were Sal at his best; they were sophisticated and instructive. Because the food had to look perfect, this forced me to be creative in more ways than one. I worked out that if I placed a bag of rice under pastry it would help make a pie sit up to look full and rounded. (I don't recommend you try this at home.) However, the best way to photograph food is right after it's been taken from the oven, still steaming hot or freshly made.

Martha Morseth, Peter and I in a trypot at Akaroa.

We grew herbs and flowers in the garden and during photo shoots, I could run outside and pick mint, coriander, a few pansies, or a bloom or two to set things off. Styling the finished dish for the camera—getting it just right—then standing back and watching Sal go to work was my favourite moment.

In order to meet our publisher's deadline, Jane and I travelled to Auckland and spent several days holed up in a hotel, putting the final touches to the text. Working under pressure seemed to bring out the best in us and we laughed and joked until the last 'T' was crossed. Even though we were both worker-bees, Jane and I still knew how to have fun.

Yet again, we found ourselves back at Avalon Studios to start filming a microwave series. Cliff had arranged another television series with TVNZ – 'Microwave Menus' was to have 13 episodes.

It was the same story with the kitchens—the *real* kitchen was out the back in the workshop area, but at least this time, we were more experienced and confident about getting what we needed. We had trolleys to help transport equipment between the studio and the work area, but Jane still found herself, more than once, out in the parking lot with a hose and a bucket, washing dishes.

We were well aware that our work-team caused a fair bit of disruption at Avalon, creating, as we did, a hive of activity. Once word got out, people dropped by from all over to see what we were doing. The atmosphere was charged and exciting. Joe Sherry, who took a great deal of interest in our preparations, ran the Avalon cafeteria. If we ran out of butter, Jane would dash up to see Joe; if we needed to refrigerate something for a few hours, Joe was always ready to oblige. We were starting to feel at home.

The New Microwave Cookbook was published in 1987. It was a handsome book and looked the way we wanted it to: professional. It turned out that Beckett Sterling was right. The book went straight to the bestseller list and sold over 160,000 copies.

In the spring of 1987, Kirsten was woken in the middle of the night by my mother banging on the wall between their flats. She rushed in to Mum's flat and immediately arranged for her grandmother to be taken to hospital. Mum, tragically, had had a stroke. Although she was active right up till then, Mum had been unwell for a while, suffering from chronic bronchitis, in spite of never having been a smoker. The bronchitis left her breathless, coughing her way through many nights. She had also developed diabetes, and of course, there were the ongoing difficulties with her hips and other ailments.

I flew down to Dunedin to be with Mum and every day went to sit with her in the hospital. She was well aware of what was going on around her, even to the point of criticising something I was knitting for Elizabeth.

But after a week, she started to slip away. Near the end, I got into bed with Mum and held her close. She was barely conscious. With her eyes closed, she began talking very quietly to her mother and her sisters who had passed away so many years before. She was moving between this world and the next. She knew where she wanted to go. It was the last gift that she gave me.

After all her illnesses and bravery, I don't think she had any strength left to carry on. She died peacefully.

While in Dunedin, I was staying at the flat with Kirsten. One afternoon, after Mum had died, we were there together when Elizabeth began running between the two flats, calling out for her 'Nana'. Her voice seemed to echo throughout the empty space. We felt unbearably sad.

One carries on, of course, but I felt a great sense of loss and deep sadness. My mother had been such a lively and vibrant part of our lives. It seemed impossible that she wasn't going to burst through the door at any moment.

This is our Lemnos Avenue house after the flat roof, which leaked, was replaced by a sloping roof. After Kirsten and Simon left home, the backyard was planted in flowers instead of being a home for all their various pets.

Lindsay Pontiflex, a good friend, kept our garden looking beautiful.

While Simon was studying in Christchurch, he came home to Lemnos Avenue during the university summer holidays. One such summer day, we were chatting in the kitchen when out of the blue, he said, 'I wish you would write a cookbook without meat.' His girlfriend, Sandra (we all call her Sam), was vegetarian and his diet had changed dramatically. He told me that his flatmates and friends found most of their vegetarian recipes in either American cookbooks or books from the UK. According to Simon, it was difficult to find New Zealand recipes for vegetarian meals. I told him I'd think about it, but then he said, 'Why don't we do it together?'

And that is what we did — over two summers. It could have been a disaster, but we were used to one another in the kitchen. Having two cooks from different generations, focused on the same thing, firing ideas at each other across the kitchen seemed to work for us. It broadened our horizons; Simon pushed me and I, naturally, challenged him. What could have been a solitary and creatively demanding task turned out to be inspiring and doubly pleasurable. Often, if one of our recipes turned out to be less than satisfactory, I couldn't wait to get up in the morning to talk to Simon about it, as usually, during the night, I'd worked out a way to make it better. And he did the same.

At that stage Kirsten and Elizabeth were staying with us because Mark was away working at a holiday job, and Peter's mother, Cassie, was staying too. All the vegetarian recipes we tested during the day were placed on the table for our evening meal. We didn't make a point of saying these are vegetarian dishes, we just served the meal. The dishes that didn't get the thumbs up from family and friends didn't get into the book. It was as simple as that.

I enjoyed the challenge that *not* cooking with meat presented. How could we get a robust-tasting risotto without using chicken stock? Could we make a flavoursome bean casserole without the addition of bacon?

Yes, of course we could, by using vegetable stocks and lots of fresh herbs and spices. Simon introduced ethnic foods to our repertoire. We wanted people to enjoy the food for what it was and not even notice that there wasn't any meat in the recipes.

Kirsten with her husband Mark Buxton and Elizabeth, 1986. Kirsten and I made her dress together.

Simon, Peter, Kirsten and me at Kirsten's wedding. I was wearing a Christian Dior, silk gown that Sharon Crosbie had helped me find in the nightwear department in Bonwit Teller's in New York.

Simon put all the recipes on the computer. Sal took the photos for the book, and Clare, who was visiting from the UK, brought her own flair to everything, including some lovely line drawings that were reproduced throughout. Jane worked right beside us, assisting at every opportunity. We had enormous fun putting this book together.

Cliff by this time had decided to strike out on his own, setting up CJ Publishing. I'd enjoyed working with Cliffy, so we decided to continue together. He'd successfully published three of my *Microwave Menu* books and released *Meals without Meat* in 1990. We held our collective breaths. Would this book work?

The book seemed to hit just the right note and became an instant bestseller. It's been kept in print for 20 years, selling well over 260,000 copies.

That year, we also decided to publish *Recipes to Remember*. I suppose, because New Zealand was looking back 150 years, I started looking back, too, over my years of cooking in public. I included recipes that were too good to forget and those that would stand the test of time.

We had such a good time putting the book together: the team of Jane, Dee and I, along with photographer, Sal Criscillo, were joined by Clare, my sister. Clare gloriously seized upon the nostalgic theme, sending us all off to fetch antique treasures as well as family photos; everything from old seed packets to a beautifully made metal egg-beater were artistically incorporated into the final design. I dedicated the book to my granddaughter, Elizabeth, who had just started to write her own name.

During this time I was still writing my 'Kitchen Diary' column. I liked the immediacy of the column and the way it made me feel connected to my readers. It hardly seemed possible that in 1989 we published *Kitchen Diary* cookbook number twelve. Two years later, INL published the *Kitchen Diary Collection,* complete with Clare's drawings. It remains one of my favourite books.

O ne hot summer day in the late 1989, I opened the door of Lemnos Avenue to a tall, smiling man who introduced himself as Bernie Crosby. He had come to talk to me about a business venture.

I took him through our house to the conservatory where we could enjoy a gentle breeze and the colour of the back garden. As we sat, enjoying a cold beer, Bernie started to talk. Little did I know then that this meeting would be the start of something that would change the way bulk foods were sold in supermarkets, and that it would be the beginning of a long friendship with Bernie and his wife Kaye.

Bernie enthusiastically told me about his business, Prolife Foods, a small family company based in Hamilton. He and his wife imported dried fruits and nuts that they sold into supermarkets and health food shops. Customers scooped out what they wanted from a collection of barrels and bins, generally known as 'bulk food departments'.

With all the charm of his Irish forefathers, Bernie explained his vision of building an exciting range of top quality, value-for-money, bulk foods. He was sure that this was what customers wanted and he wanted to brand the bulk foods with my name.

Bernie and I batted ideas back and forth all afternoon. We talked about developing a food club for customers, sending out regular newsletters, having free recipes available in each store, doing fund-raising cooking demonstrations around the country and designing bins and scoops that were easier for customers to use. The rest is history. Alison's Choice, now Alison's Pantry, has become a major player in supermarkets throughout New Zealand.

Early on, I began working with Russelle Knaap from Prolife and our friendship continues till the present day. We worked together on everything from the publication of recipes, the preparation of newsletters, store visits, food shows and product development, as well as publicity.

The conservatory at Lemnos Avenue.

The fund-raising cooking shows sponsored by Alison's Choice gave me great satisfaction. For a number of years we did 12 shows a year, raising money for Child Cancer, Plunket, primary and secondary schools, civic groups and kindergartens, and we raised many thousands of dollars.

The groups we worked with were all so different. Some were good at selling tickets but not so good on organisation. Others were perfect organisers but forgot to sell tickets, and sometimes, they were good at both. I was usually relieved when we reached the end of the show and everything had run smoothly, because many of the groups had never attempted anything like this before.

To make things easier, we developed a step by step list of instructions on how to set up the stage, how to prepare ingredients, instruct helpers, and sell tickets for the show. Everything was laid out in such precise detail that I could arrive in the afternoon of D Day, have a quick run through with my on-stage helpers, then get ready for the main event.

Russelle made sure that the organisers were doing everything according to our instructions. She would be in constant contact with them for several weeks beforehand to ensure the night would be a success. Over time she developed a kind of 'radar' and could sense when all was not well, despite assurances to the contrary.

One afternoon, while we were driving to a town for a show that night, we received a phone call. We had had a very successful show the night before with over 600 tickets sold. Russelle took the call and I could see her face change. Tonight's group had only sold 60 tickets! They had barely sold enough to cover their costs, and they were seriously worried.

'No problem,' Russelle assured them. 'We'll fix it.' She pulled over to the side of the road, rang directory service, got the number of the local radio station and called them.

'I've got Alison Holst in the car. We are coming to town tonight to do a fundraising cooking show. Would you like to talk to her on air?' Russelle handed the phone over to me and started up the car. As the green fields flashed by, I talked about our cooking show and told listeners where to buy tickets. By the time we arrived, several hours later, almost 300 tickets had been sold. We had a lovely show, raised a fair bit of money for charity and everyone was pleased.

Kaye and Bernie Crosby with me in front of the 'Alison's Pantry' section of the Orewa supermarket, 2011.

Russelle and I spent many hours on the road together and although we always resolved 'to save our voices for the night', we invariably talked and laughed and talked some more. I look back on these trips with great pleasure.

For me, Alison's Pantry is very special. It has been really satisfying to see the way the business has developed and evolved from a few simple products in bins and barrels, to more than 200 varied and interesting products. When I walk through a supermarket and see row upon row of gleaming bins, filled to the brim with the colourful, fresh foods that carry my name, I feel a real sense of pride.

Having a rest while walking near wheat fields in England, 1980.

Chapter **eleven:**

Cakes and Quilts

In 1989, Peter obtained a leave of absence for five months to allow us to travel. Some time before our departure, I'd sat beside a young man on a flight to Dunedin. He was upset because he had flown from England to New Zealand to see his girlfriend who told him, after he had arrived, that she wanted him to go away! I sympathised with him, but when I told him that we were looking for a house to rent in England, he said that his mother had a cottage near Kingsbridge in Devon. We contacted her and arranged to stay there for two months. We then spent about two months in Lancaster, house-sitting for friends, made a side trip to Switzerland to see the Junods, and had a week in France on a barge with Clare, Ian and the Hickeys. We also visited friends in Scotland at Loch Drambhuie. Peter's father died a few weeks before our planned return and we came back for his funeral.

While we were away, Peter came to the realisation that the demands of the hospital were taking a toll. Although he'd enjoyed his professional life, he didn't wish to continue working at the same, relentless pace. Eventually, in 1993, at the ripe old age of 55, he retired from his full-time position, and took various short-term hospital locum positions for several years.

After her graduation from the University of Otago, Kirsten and Mark both took jobs in Palmerston North. We liked having them live within a few hours from us. In 1992, our second granddaughter, Jennifer, was born. She was a dear little dark-haired girl, very unlike her fair sister, Elizabeth.

When Simon finished university, he applied for a job at Crop and Food Research near Lincoln University. The position offered the right combination for him — research and practical work testing wheat. By this time, we'd already published our book *Meals without Meat*, and apparently, that helped him get the job; knowing the basic principles of baking a loaf of bread seemed to be an essential requirement.

In 1995, Simon and Sam decided to travel overseas for a year. They had a wonderful time back packing through Europe, taking in the markets and local foods along the way. Simon also called in to see Clare in London and ended up working as an assistant on some of her food styling projects.

When the children were young, I often took them with me when visiting exotic food stores and market places like Ocean Commodities in Wellington. Simon remembers the lively atmosphere of these places and how I always asked the different vendors about the unfamiliar foods. Over time, this had become an ingrained practice for him, too. His interest in ethnic foods increased dramatically after their trip.

When Sam and Simon returned to New Zealand in 1996, Sam got a job in Wellington and they decided to move there. Before moving, they were married in the Chapel of Christchurch Hospital — the same hospital where my mother had trained as a nurse many years before. We had a great family gathering in Christchurch to celebrate their wedding.

Sandra (Ford) and Simon were married in Christchurch in 1997.

In 1991, Cliff masterminded a mammoth task for 'Team Alison'. He wanted us to put together my favourite recipes, over 1000 of them, along with tips for everything under the sun, and publish it as *The Best of Alison Holst*, a book we all later referred to as 'the Big Red Book'.

It was a huge undertaking, and I hired Hillary Wilson-Hill to help compile the recipes. We put Hillary in a room upstairs at Lemnos Avenue and it was her job to put all the recipes together, in order.

Jane, Dee and I, along with Sal, rolled up our collective sleeves and set to work. The recipes were chosen from all the books I'd published thus far. It turned out to be an expansive, 320 page, full-colour book jointly published by CJ Publishing and Hodder Moa Beckett.

Whenever we were working on a book project, the most exciting time of the day was at 10 a.m. when the courier arrived. We'd all sit down to look at the trannies from the previous day's photo shoot. Closely examining these colourful little gems helped spur us on for the day ahead.

Sal and I chose the photos. I preferred ones that showed the natural vibrancy of food: the deep, intense red of a sliced tomato embedded proudly in a cheesy quiche or the gleaming, golden skin of a well-roasted chicken. We loved the warmth that a steaming bowl of soup conveyed or the freshness of a just tossed, green salad. It was immensely pleasing when we got everything right. With food photography, you want the finished dish to look delicious and attractive; so much so, that it inspires people to *get cooking*.

I've probably received more letters and emails about 'the Big Red Book' than any other book I've written. It's been reprinted many times and is still in print today. Most of the letters are from women who tell me they've just given a copy to one of their children because they've left home, or they've replaced theirs with a new copy, as the old one was falling apart. I can't tell you how satisfying it is, at this stage in my career, to receive such letters. I get a kick out of the fact that people are enjoy my books.

Cliff and I continued to publish various books together well into the 90s. In 1993, we published *Family Favourites*, then went on to produce *Breakfasts and Brunches*, *Good Food*, and in 1997, a little book about economical meals for families, *Dollars and Sense*. In 1998 Cliff sold me to New Holland publishers. At least, that was the way I saw it. I had no idea I could be sold, but suddenly CJ Publishing no longer existed and the books that Cliff and I did together now belonged to New Holland.

🖘 *Email received 30 July 2011*

Dear Alison,

For some time I have been meaning to write and say thank you. Many years ago, when I had little children, I would listen to your slot on National Radio. I think it was a Thursday morning, and for me it was a window of sanity. Your down-to-earth approach and interesting and informative chats with Sharon Crosbie would not only educate me, but also take me outside the walls of our home. I enjoyed preparing food for the family, but you often fired my imagination to do something a bit differently. In future years I actually had my own small catering business. One broadcast I remember particularly well! (Sept 1990.) You had given the recipe for Peter's birthday cake. I was heavily pregnant, and as I listened, I thought, well that would be a nice cake to make for the family to enjoy especially if I was to have the baby soon. I got some of the ingredients out onto the bench, then had a contraction. Knowing my labour history, already having 3 children, I put everything away, rang my husband at work, and 3 hours later we had our 2nd daughter. So Peter's birthday cake recipe has significant memories for me.

So thank you for the many helpful tips, suggestions, recipes, recipe books and bringing another world into my kitchen, on days when I sometimes felt overwhelmed with domesticity. I so appreciate your homely approach, taking the mystery out of food preparation for thousands of New Zealanders.

I have endeavoured to educate my family in the kitchen: one daughter became a chef and our other children are all confident cooks.

With my sincere and grateful regards.

Julia Burnett

☞ *Email received 26 November 2010*

> Hi – I bought your book, *The Best of Alison Holst*, 20 years ago when I
> had my first child. I have three now. I love your book. When we hadn't
> much money it was the best book to use. I had a friend in New York
> who worked for a large publisher and she sent me all the posh cook-
> books. They are still in perfect order, not like yours. It has no cover,
> burn and scorch marks up the side. When I was making plum jam,
> pages fell out and I named them and put them into envelopes. The
> microwave choc cake recipe is so faint you can hardly see the words. I
> just love your book. When I saw it on special at PaperPlus this week, I
> thought I'll get myself a new one. I think it will only weigh half as much
> 'cause it won't have any ingredients spilled on it. Thank you so much
> for helping me through some tough times and making my kids very
> happy. You are much more than you will know to a lot of people.
>
> XX Teryl

When Simon and Sam came to live in Wellington, he and I started talking about the future. It seemed perfectly natural for us to start working together. Simon had obviously been inspired, not only by the success of *Meals without Meat*, but by his travels through Europe and the variety of different foods he'd encountered. I was heartened by his enthusiasm and was quite chuffed that he took so much interest in what I was doing.

In many ways, having Simon join me was a continuation of what we'd always done. Cooking in our family is considered a fundamental life skill. But having my son in the kitchen with me certainly helped revitalise and energise me, and my working life.

Simon reckons he and I are 'alarmingly similar' in many ways. There's some of both of us in every book we do and we think our books are better as a result. We're similar in our approach to food; we both prefer gentle persuasion to brow-beating. We'd sooner lead people quietly and willingly towards an improved diet. Softly, softly seems to work best for us.

....

When my first book, *Here's How*, was published in 1966, John Hyndman, the owner of Hyndman's Bookshop, invited me to cook in his shop window. His store was ideally placed on the main street of Dunedin, near the Octagon, and to my surprise, we drew quite a crowd. Even one of my neighbours, Wanda Hall, came in to ask me to sign her copy. I was so new at this sort of thing that I didn't know what to write. She suggested 'Best wishes and good cooking', a salutation I use to this day.

Because Mr Hyndman was the first person to take an interest, I always made a point of going in to see him whenever I was in Dunedin. He was one of the early, innovative booksellers, always organising functions to help promote books.

One day when I called by to say hello, Mr Hyndman's son, Neil, was working in the store. We started chatting and out of the blue, Neil suggested that I write a muffin cookbook. I wasn't so sure. 'Aren't there a lot of them about?' I asked.

We continued with our conversation, but as I was leaving the shop, Neil again raised the idea of a muffin book. 'Are you *sure* you don't think it would be a good idea?'

'Oh, maybe I will. I'll give it some thought', I replied.

Neil paused and then asked, 'And who would you get to publish it?'

'Well, Neil, it's your idea. Do you want to publish it?'

I can still see the look on his face. Neil looked so delighted that I thought, well, maybe it would be a good idea. I went home, put on my apron and started to research muffins. They're an American invention that I remembered well from our time in California. Scones are the Kiwi equivalent, but muffins were, in many ways, considered a healthy alternative to most cakes and sweets. A basic muffin is quick and easy to make and the variations are endless.

I put together a little book called *Marvellous Muffins*. I ate so many muffins while testing the recipes for this book that I thought I might turn into one! It was published under Hyndman Publishing in 1994. At first, Neil thought printing 5000 copies would be about right, but the response from the book trade was astonishingly positive, so he printed double that number. However, my little muffin book surpassed all expectations, hitting the bestseller lists for months on end. It's been an enormously popular book and it is still in print today, having sold 280,000 copies thus far.

The book also cemented my relationship with Neil. We enjoyed working together; I found him an enthusiastic, hard-working publisher, who, after all his years of working in a bookshop, had good instincts about the types of books people were looking for. Our next project was another best seller, *Best Potato Recipes*. The popularity of these books extended to Australia, where we've sold many, many copies.

The success of the books led to the sale of the Hyndman family bookshop which then allowed Neil to follow a career in publishing. We went on to publish many more books together. They were neither big nor expensive, but practical books that seemed to meet a need. And once Simon came to work with me on a more permanent basis, Neil published many of our co-authored titles: a soup cookbook, a bread book, one on easy chicken recipes and even a cookbook about baby food.

Sometimes, when I was in London, Clare's agent would ask me to do some food styling if Clare was already committed to something else. I loved doing this and was more than happy to pitch in. These assignments were varied and quite exciting. On one occasion, the film director of a TV commercial asked me to come along a day early so that I could see the enormous china bowl he wanted filled with Christmas cake batter.

When I got back to our place — at the time, Peter and I were staying close to Hyde Park in a flat on the fourth floor — I went shopping for all the ingredients I needed. By the time I had carried everything home, then up four flights of stairs, I was cursing the Christmas cake. I'd estimated that in order to fill the big bowl, I'd need at least enough ingredients to make four cakes.

I spent many hours creaming and mixing the four batches of batter. Then I put all the cake batter together into a very large, plastic bag and set off to the studio. When we tipped the mixture into the big bowl, it was a perfect fit.

The director had arranged for a child to stand behind the bowl, holding a wooden spoon. Simple enough, but when he asked the child to lick the spoon, she was horrified and became quite upset. The poor child had to be calmed by her mother, who assured her daughter that she'd find the batter tasted quite nice.

After everything was finally 'in the can' and we were clearing up, I was invited to join the director and others for lunch. I was told to throw the uncooked cake mixture out. I couldn't bear the waste so I put it back into the plastic bag and took it to the restaurant. It was somewhat embarrassing preventing this large bag and its contents from oozing out beneath my chair during lunch.

I carried my big bag all the way home, up the stairs to the flat and baked the lot in two large roasting pans. We enjoyed these delicious cakes for several weeks.

Clare at Guildford, UK 1988.

Patricia with her cat, London, 1987.

It was fascinating to see how different TV studios worked and even more so to see my sister in action. The budgets of the different projects Clare worked on were far more generous and flamboyant than anything we'd ever experienced in New Zealand. Once, I helped out on a movie set, making the cucumber sandwiches for a wedding breakfast scene in the film *Eye of the Needle*, starring the handsome Christopher Cazenove. Clare and I always had a lot of fun together.

I once took Mum on one of my trips to the UK. She loved it! Clare whizzed Mum around London in her dashing little sports car while poor Mum held on for dear life, terrified by having to sit down low, close to the road. She stayed with Patricia and David in their lovely home and thoroughly enjoyed the sights of London, going off on picnics and watching Londoners going about their daily business.

While I was inspired by North American cooking, Clare has always been drawn to the vibrant cuisines of Europe. She now works as a food consultant for companies as diverse as Sainsbury's and Bacardi, as well as a food stylist for all the top-rated advertising agencies working on TV commercials. Clare writes regular articles and features for *Homes & Gardens*, and has contributed to all the major magazines: everything from *Elle* to *Wallpaper*. She's worked with Nigella Lawson, the 'Two Fat Ladies', and many others, and has had over 20 splendid cookbooks published: her titles include *A Taste of Morocco*, *Flavours of Provence* and *Rice: From Risotto to Sushi*.

Clare is an exuberant, creative and very clever 'foodie'. She's very much at home in Italy, France and England. Clare and Ian also share a little holiday cottage in Greece. Recently, they purchased a house in the South Island where they now hope to spend the northern hemisphere winters. It's a lovely villa with a large veranda that faces the sea.

Both my sisters have enjoyed exceptional success abroad. Patricia has retired from singing now, but her distinguished operatic career spanned over 40 years. She has performed in all the great opera houses around the world. She joined Pavarotti on stage over one hundred times and sang

We sisters three, Clare, me and Patricia very tanned, London, 1986.

with the likes of Kiri Te Kanawa, Montserrat Caballé, Placido Domingo and José Carreras. She's worked with many great conductors: Zubin Mehta, Sir Neville Mariner and Sir John Pritchard to mention a few. In 2001 Patricia was appointed Officer of the New Zealand Order of Merit for her contributions to opera and the community, and in 2007 she was awarded an Honorary Doctorate of Music from the University of Otago.

Now Patricia's passions include painting and fly fishing, both of which she does with great skill and artistry. Her paintings are sold through an Auckland gallery and one of her exquisite fish paintings graces the wall in my study at home. She enjoys teaching singing and fundraising for charity. Patricia and her husband David now live in our old neighbourhood of Opoho, just around the corner from our Blacks Road home, where we grew up.

Patricia proudly holds her 2011 early morning catch! A 14 pound trout from the Clutha River, Central Otago.

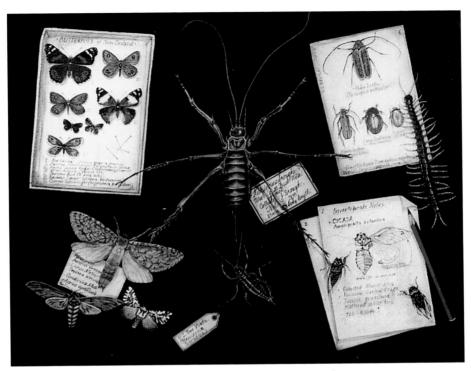

'New Zealand Entomologist's Table Top' by Patricia Payne, 2009. [Private collection, Auckland.]

On one of my early trips to Canada, George Hanson, who was chief executive of the New Zealand Lamb Company, and his wife, Donna, kindly invited me to stay at their home in Toronto for a few days, before I started my work for the Meat Board. I admired one of Donna's beautiful handcrafted quilts and she offered to take me to a local quilting shop.

It was the most wonderful store—filled with colour and fabulous fabrics. I instantly wanted to make a quilt of my own. I chose about a dozen different fabrics, some patterned and some plain. The store owner asked me what size quilt I wanted to make and then, without a second thought, she cut strips of fabric for me. I worried that I might not have enough material, but I needn't have any qualms. When my quilt was finished there were only a few scraps of fabric left.

I also bought some wadding, plenty of a creamy-white fabric and a 'lap quilting' frame that measured about 40 cm square. For the next few years, whenever I flew long distances, I took the frame and my quilting fabrics with me so I could stitch happily for hours on end.

Each time I finished a square I'd put it in my suitcase and start on the next piece. Deciding on the design of the new square gave me the most pleasure. Sometimes I used a traditional pattern, but mostly I liked to depict something that would remind me of the places where I'd been.

For my first quilt I designed a square with maple leaves to honour my first visit to Canada. Memories of my mother inspired the teapot and scones square. I sewed a small pocket inside the teapot so I could hide treats for my grandchildren.

The red poppies square was prompted by the many walks Peter and I have had through wheat fields in England. Often while there, we'd climb over a stile to find a much-used diagonal path through the golden wheat and red poppies.

In one corner of my quilt is a little house with two trees standing behind it. This represents our place at Manakau. Peter planted two redwood trees behind our house that have grown enormously tall since I first stitched this square. This design reminds me of the many times we have walked and camped in the redwood forests of California.

Before our Manakau house was built, we'd 'camp' in a double garage on the property. One summer, during the strawberry season, Kirsten and her friends picked strawberries as a holiday job and we all stayed in the garage. While they were away picking strawberries all day, I spent a peaceful time sewing a strawberry design for my quilt, making strawberry jam and gardening.

The fleur-de-lis, the ancient emblem of Florence, reminds me of the time Patricia and I were there. I've included Hawaiian motifs, a 'Big Apple' to represent New York; a stylised medal that reminds me of the time I was honoured by the Queen; a rooster to remind me of our hens, and a symbol from one of the banners we saw when Peter and I went to the Fourth International Horticultural Exhibition in Munich.

In the middle of my quilt is a picture of Peter, with one arm around me and a spade in his other hand. I am holding a basket filled with the vegetables he grows and which the whole family eats with great enjoyment. ▪

Peter and I walking along the beach at Orewa.

Chapter **twelve:**

Life's a Beach

To celebrate the new millennium, New Holland asked me to produce *The Ultimate Cookbook*, a weighty tome. It became known as the 'Big Gold Book' and was to be a companion volume to the 'Big Red Book'. It came as quite a surprise to me, at the time, that it would be my eightieth book.

That realisation made me stop in my tracks and take stock. In so many ways, this book represented a goodly portion of my life. It ended up being a personal collection of the recipes I liked best and the ones that I used in my own kitchen. In the introduction, I wrote, 'I hope my children and grandchildren will hunt through this book for their personal favourites and smile as particular recipes remind them of the many happy times we have had together—in my kitchen, around various dining tables, in the garden, at a picnic or camp site—enjoying the food as well as the company of friends and extended family.' This was the same experience I wanted for those home cooks who used my recipes: family and friends celebrating good times and good food.

Sam, Rufus, Isabella and Simon in their garden, December, 1998.

Simon and I continued to work steadily with Neil Hyndman and still do to this day. The three of us have great fun throwing ideas around. Neil always comes up with interesting concepts and listens carefully to ours. We make a good team. Once we agree on a title, Simon and I start experimenting. We've worked on several book series that concentrate on quick and easy meals and desserts, in addition to a series of cookbooks with '100' recipes — everything from muffins and slices to 'twenty minute' dishes. Often the topics of our books reflect Simon's own circumstances at home, hence *Baby Food and Beyond* (which included photos of Simon's young children), and *School Lunches*.

The idea for one of our bestselling titles came from a retailer, Tony Mores, who at that time was working for the Paper Plus bookstore chain. Neil often chatted to people in the book trade, seeking out 'intelligence' at the coal face. Tony Mores suggested a 'slow cooker' cookbook. At first, the three of us were a bit lukewarm about the idea. I'd been introduced to slow cookers while travelling overseas, but I'd only ever used them occasionally. However, we were always open to new ideas so we ran with it. Simon and I started tackling cooking with a slow cooker and soon we were hooked. When used correctly, slow cookers proved to be another brilliant, time-saving appliance.

Our *100 Great Ways to use Slow Cookers* went straight to the bestseller list and stayed there. Two years later, we wrote another companion volume, *Year Round Ways to Use Slow Cookers*, and it did the same thing. One never knows how well a book will do out in the marketplace. Sometimes the timing is just right. Our third slow cooker book, published this year, is as popular as the earlier books.

Simon and I also hold demonstrations together at food shows and fund raisers. These are great fun to do, but certainly require a lot of organisation beforehand—some things never change. Often we appear together in the media, either because we've published a book on, say, breadmaking, or because we've been invited to cook on television. Even so, Simon is far more active than I am these days. He has his own independent working life and so do I.

....

In September, 2001, Kirsten asked me to come to Palmerston North to stay with her and the girls. She and Mark had separated.

I left for Palmerston North immediately, but as soon as I arrived, Peter rang to tell us to turn on the TV. It was September 11, 2001. The Twin Towers of the World Trade Center in New York had been attacked. Like most people, we were stunned by the images of these giant skyscrapers collapsing into dust and ash.

Dear Grandma,

Thank-you so much for having me to stay. I've had a really lovely time having you all to myself, and doing all of the things I remember so well.

Love + kisses, Liz.

From left, my Aunty Ini, Uncle Jack, Aunty Nell's widower, and Aunty Kath.

The destructive scenes we watched conjured up World War II memories from my own childhood. I remembered watching fighter planes conduct a military exercise over our peaceful home on Blacks Road, how my Aunty had returned from the war, seriously unwell, and how my uncle had lost part of his hand.

The New York tragedy we witnessed abruptly brought things into perspective for us. Peter and I helped Kirsten where we could, finding that, before long, she carried on with her usual enthusiasm, working at the hospital and raising her two lovely daughters. She is an amazingly resourceful woman, and I am very proud of her.

....

In December, 1993, a friend who lived in Takapuna called, asking us if we'd house-sit for a week or so, while she and her husband went sailing. We jumped at the chance. Peter no longer had hospital commitments and the weather in Wellington that summer had been appalling: windy, wet and cold.

We drove to Takapuna and immediately found ourselves bathed in warm, balmy sunshine. We walked along the beach, swam in the warm water and relaxed in the sun. Sea breezes wafted through my friend's comfortable house. We loved it! The summer weather was a tonic to us hunched-against-the-wind Wellingtonians.

Peter and I set off on day trips to explore the nearby beaches and regional parks. We were so taken by the Whangaparoa Peninsula that we bought a section that was just a stone's throw away from a sheltered beach. We thought it would be the perfect spot to build a house.

Not long after our Takapuna stay, both Peter and I were working in Auckland at the same time. I had a demonstration scheduled in Orewa, so we booked a motel there for a few nights. Come Sunday morning, we walked along the beach and spotted a couple of 'for sale' signs. When we got back to the motel, Peter said, 'You know, it would be much easier to buy a house instead of building one.' I admitted that I, too, had been having second thoughts about building on our section. I suggested we ring the land agent.

'I can't show you the houses until tomorrow because the owners need more notice. But I do have an apartment I could show you straight away,' he said.

'We aren't interested in buying an apartment,' I replied.

'Why not look anyway,' he said. 'The apartment I'm talking about is directly over the road from you, and I'm there now — why don't you come over?'

Peter suggested I go and have a look at it. What did I have to lose?

I rang the doorbell, and the agent came out to meet me. The entrance hall was rather dark and gloomy, causing me to mutter something about it being like a rabbit hole. 'Keep going,' he said, and I did.

Another door opened and, suddenly, I was standing in a large, sunny space with floor-to-ceiling windows and glass doors, looking out onto a large lawn and a picture-book beach. To the right was the Whangaparaoa Peninsula, and beyond it the Coromandel Peninsula. To my left was Kawau Island, and in the distance, Great Barrier and Little Barrier Islands. The sea glinted in the sunlight, and I knew instantly that I could live here. It was stunningly beautiful.

Peter liked the apartment just as much as I did, so we bought it on the spot! We soon sold our land on the Whangaparaoa Peninsula, and for a few years, we travelled back and forth between Wellington and Orewa, often bringing our children and grandchildren with us. Eventually we sold our Wellington house in 2005 and moved to Orewa to live permanently.

Often, when Kirsten was working, our granddaughters, Liz and Jen, spent their school holidays with us at Orewa. We loved having their lively, bouncy presence in our home. They enjoyed walking on the beach and exploring the rock pools, swimming in the sea and relaxing in the sun. They still do.

Three generations of Otago graduates; Kirsten, Elizabeth and me photographed in front of the clock tower at the University of Otago.

When they were younger they liked to sit on my lap while I read them stories, or when I was cross-stitching; they also liked to help me in the kitchen with baking. Once, I offered to teach Liz how to cross-stitch but she replied, 'No thanks, I just love sitting here with your arms around me while you sew.' I feel very close to my granddaughters, and I value their friendship now that they're adults. They keep in touch by email on a weekly basis, and Jen recently came to stay with me for a week to help put my archives in order. Jen is now at Massey studying zoology, and her older sister, Liz, is working in London as a lawyer.

Simon's children, Isabella and Theo, enjoy visiting Orewa, too. Both children started swimming when they were babies and are now excellent swimmers, just like their father. They love the fact that the beach is right outside our front door. When Bella's playing in the surf, her long, blonde hair streams behind her, making her look just like a little mermaid. Theo has now mastered riding a surfboard — he seems to be growing up very quickly.

....

We love living at Orewa. The sound and smell of the sea greet us every morning. Spotting kingfishers or watching gannets ride the waves brings us endless pleasure. We love being able to walk everywhere we need to go. Often our shopping trips take longer than we plan because we're always stopping to chat to people. Shopkeepers call out to tell me that the book I ordered has arrived or just to say hello. The local librarian always has time to talk.

One day, I told the helpful women at the bank that I enjoy dealing with an 'all-woman' bank. 'We do have one man here,' they said, 'but we keep him out the back.'

A few months after we came to live in Orewa, I happened to meet Thomas Cook, a local artist, in the chemist shop. We were both in the photographic area, trying to choose which photos to have printed. In passing, Thomas told me he was going to be speaking to an Orewa art class and planned to use photos to illustrate his talk.

My ears perked up — an art class was exactly what I wanted! Thomas promised to give my name and phone number to the woman in charge of the class.

A few days later, Jane Jenson called me. She was warm and enthusiastic and told me about the art class she was running. It sounded perfect! Jane invited me to join her class at the Orewa Community Church Hall on Tuesday afternoon. When I arrived, I was given a warm welcome, as is every newcomer.

Elizabeth Buxton

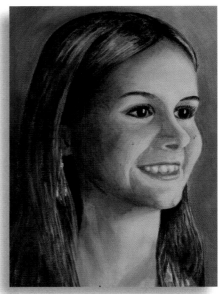

Jennifer Buxton

Isabella Holst

Theo Holst

Inspired by my art class, I painted these portraits of my grandchildren.

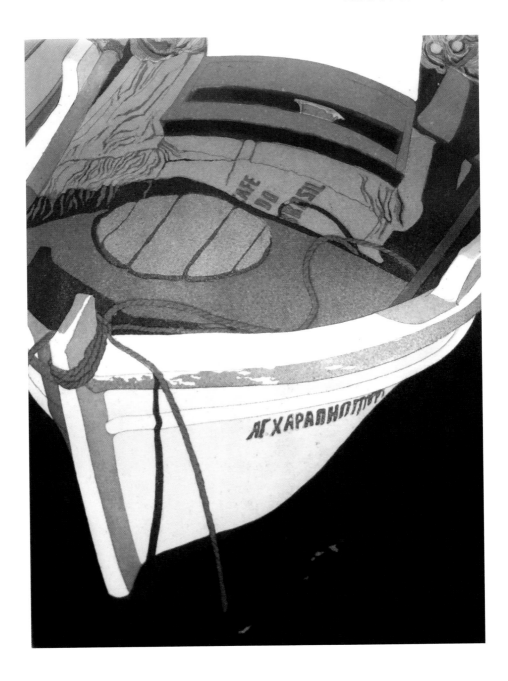

'Barka' (Greek for boat), an etching by Clare Ferguson, 1982.

In the years since, the time I spend at Jane's art class has become one of the highlights of my week. There is such a happy buzz in the room as we draw, paint, talk, swap notes and admire each other's work. Our class is in its seventh year. Jane encourages us to try painting in different mediums; I started with watercolours using my old box of watercolour paints from H.V. Miller's class, although I have added a few different colours to the range.

Jane has taught me how to become more proficient with other mediums too: pastels, acrylics, Genesis and oils. At the moment, my favourite medium is acrylics, which I use to paint landscapes, but who knows what I might try next month. Jane tells me that I have encouraged some of the more reticent painters in our class. Maybe my excitement about each new thing is infectious. I hope that this is so!

Every week, everyone in our art class donates two dollars towards funding the purchase of art supplies for children in Fiji. It's a wonderful initiative that we all feel strongly about.

My sketch of a house in Eureka, California.

Simon holding Theo; me; Peter holding Rufus, and Sandra holding Isabella at our garden at Manakau.

When Simon and Sam left for their trip overseas in 1995, they left their wire-haired terrier with us. Rufus most definitely had a mind of his own. I like to think he enjoyed living with us; Peter and I usually took him for a walk every morning, and, as I was at home during the day, he got plenty of attention. It didn't take us long to fall hopelessly in love with Rufus.

We always took a tennis ball on our walks as Rufus was an enthusiastic retriever. Occasionally, he'd decide that it was time for Peter and me to do some retrieving. He'd grab the ball, climb up a steep bank, wait until we were standing at the bottom of the bank, then drop the ball down to us. Rufus would play this game for as long as we would obey.

When Simon and Sam returned to Christchurch after their travels, I somewhat reluctantly took Rufus back to them. I came home to a house that seemed very quiet and empty. Some months later, when Simon and Sam returned to live in Wellington, they naturally brought Rufus with them. He'd come along to work with Simon at our house during the day and then go home with him most nights, although sometimes he'd decide to spend the night with us.

Often, in the evenings, Simon would hold Rufus in his arms for hours at a time. Obviously, he was a much loved dog. Things changed, however, when Simon and Sam's daughter, lovely little Isabella, was born. Rufus became jealous of her, particularly when she lay in Simon's arms. We agreed that Rufus would live with Peter and me.

When we made the move to Orewa, Rufus came too. He loved our early morning beach walks and retrieving toys from the sea. When Kirsten's daughters came to stay with us during the school holidays, Rufus thought life was even better.

He was a comfort-loving dog. As he got older, Peter built steps so he could climb up easily onto his special living room chair, and he'd lie there for hours. If Peter sat down on the couch, though, Rufus would climb stiffly down from his chair and wait for Peter to lift him onto the couch. Once there, he would put his head on Peter's knee, staying put for as long as Peter did.

I made Rufus a 'Huffy Puff', after the Dr Seuss book: 'I sleep in a bed with a big Huffy Puff. Come over and stay, we have Huff Puffs enough.' I filled a two-metre square cotton envelope with goose down that was given to me by an aunt. This was Rufus's bed, although he was fond of getting into bed with us if the night was cold.

The Huffy Puff would be transferred to the back of the car when we were going for a trip of several hours. If Rufus stood up, we knew he needed a comfort stop. He had us very well trained!

One sad day, while travelling to our little house at Manakau, we realised that Rufus was failing. We rang Kirsten in Palmerston North, who had been expecting us to visit her, and explained the situation. She dropped everything, picked up her doctor's bag and in half an hour was with us.

We put Rufus on his Huffy Puff and he lay there quietly. Kirsten checked his heart regularly, and eventually said, 'He's got two more minutes to live. Why don't you both stroke him quietly during this time.'

This is what we did, and in two minutes, just as she said, Rufus stopped breathing.

We buried him in the garden, covering his grave with pink camellia blossoms. We haven't yet felt that we are ready to have another dog. Although we have loved all our pets, we thought that our beloved Rufus was an extra-special family member. We will never forget him.

....

In 2009, Kirsten announced that she and John Matthews were to marry. My family likes nothing better than a big family gathering, especially a wedding. Kirsten and I set to work and had a lovely time, not only sewing her wedding dress (an ivory silk gown), but eight 'flapper' dresses for the 'attendants': nieces, granddaughters and daughters of cousins. John is from Napier, so the Art Deco theme was chosen to 'bring Napier to Palmerston North'.

The eight 'flapper' dresses that Kirsten and I made for her bridesmaids when she and John Matthews married in 2009.

Kirsten's marriage to John Matthews, Feb, 2009. Top left: Kirsten and John Matthews at the time of their engagement. Top right: Peter and I escorting Kirsten down the aisle, flanked by

Olly (poodle) and Bebe (Bichon-poodle). Below: the 'Flappers'. This page. Top: John, Kirsten and families. Bottom: bridal party and vintage car.

Everyone was involved in one way or another. Liz and Jen were the bridesmaids, and John's two eldest sons made up the boys' side. Even Kirsten's dogs were outfitted in smart waistcoats. They, along with Peter and me, led Kirsten down the aisle. Kirsten had sewn pockets into the dogs' coats where she put special favours for all the attendants: greenstone pendants for the boys (with an outline of Mahia etched on each), rings for Jen and Liz, made from an assortment of melted-down antique family rings, and bracelets and heart charms for the other girls.

Simon made the communion bread, and the communion wine came from Ken and Patricia Graham's Hitchen Road Winery at Pokeno. During the service, Simon read the introduction from my 'Big Gold Book' as well as a lesson from the Bible. Kirsten and John also included a passage from a book written by Robert B. Parker, which reflected what they think about families sharing good food and good times together. The church choir, the same one that Kirsten sings in, sang a blessing at the end of the service.

The reception was held in the church hall, which has since been demolished. As it was a bit run-down, Kirsten and I made wall hangings, in keeping with the Art Deco theme, to smarten things up. John and Kirsten constructed a gold, three-tiered cake stand, a creation of true beauty, which held the 220 cupcakes that Patricia, Clare and I helped decorate.

Without doubt, it was a memorable wedding!

....

Kirsten's husband, John, has a beach house at the base of Mahia Peninsula. Last year, Kirsten drove Peter and me to Mahia, so we could see the area for ourselves. It was warm and sunny when we arrived, prompting Kirsten and me to go swimming on the southern side of the peninsula.

We walked into the water gradually, since we weren't brave enough to dive straight in. As we laughed and called out to each other, we noticed

My watercolour of Mahia Peninsula.

a dolphin swimming towards us. The animal was obviously friendly and bumped against us gently. Since he was quite large, I worried that he might push me over, but Kirsten assured me that he could be trusted. He'd come to see her on several previous occasions.

Later in the day, John put his boat in the water, and we all went out to see if there were any fish in the net he had set earlier. We caught several fish, but when we started to head back to the beach, the dolphin reappeared, swimming right beside the boat on the side where Kirsten was sitting. She stroked him several times, then he disappeared, only to resurface a few minutes later. Again, he went straight to Kirsten, but, this time, he brought her a gift—a live seahorse that he dropped gently into her hand. She jumped into the water with the dolphin, and they swam about playfully for about ten minutes. As soon as Kirsten climbed back into the boat, the dolphin swam away, and we didn't see him again.

Kirsten has a special affinity with animals, unlike anyone I've ever known. It's a gift that has been apparent ever since her childhood; she's always been calm, quiet and kind around animals. She and John have built a new home, just outside Palmerston North, that they've called, quite fittingly, 'The Ark'. The plan is to have two of a kind of all resident animals.

....

Early this year, I was named a Dame Companion of the New Zealand Order of Merit. I had previously received a Q.S.M. (Queen's Service Medal) and a C.B.E. (Commander of the Order of the British Empire) for services to the community, as well as an Honorary Doctorate of Science from the University of Otago in 1997. However, this honour was particularly special to me.

'Kirsten and John's Ark' hangs at the entrance of their five acre block on the outskirts of Palmerston North. Kirsten asked me to paint this sign. She plans to eventually have all the animals depicted living on their farmlet.

My family joins me at Government House. From left: Jennifer, Kirsten, Peter, Isabella, me, the Right Honourable Sir Anand Satyanand, Lady Susan Satyanand, Simon and Theo at my investiture, 2011. Woolf Photography, Wellington.

My recent Honour was announced on New Year's Day, 2011. That morning, I went to the Orewa supermarket early. While I was halfway down one of the aisles, busily filling my shopping basket, the owner of the store presented me with a bouquet of flowers. Many of the other customers and staff stopped me for a hug or a quick word. It was very touching and reminded me yet again of why I love living in Orewa.

The investiture was held in Government House. Peter, Kirsten, Jennifer, along with Simon, Theo and Bella were there with me. Shortly before the ceremony, I was whisked off to the newly refurbished kitchen by the chef, Simon Peacock. He surprised me by asking me to autograph a copy of my first book, *Here's How*, which he had bought many years ago. I signed it 'Best wishes and good cooking, Alison Holst.' Goodness, I felt as though I had come full circle!

The chef told me that he'd found the prospect of cooking for me a 'bit daunting' but he'd put Central Otago rabbit on the menu in my honour.

Afterwards, we went to Simon and Sam's house for a party. They had invited many of our friends and family to join in the celebration. It was wonderful, although somewhat overwhelming, to be surrounded by the people I'd worked with and those who had supported me throughout the years. I felt very honoured indeed.

One usually ends a cookbook with an index. With this book, I'd like to end with a request.

In many schools throughout New Zealand, home economics is a forgotten subject. The cooking rooms, along with the sewing and woodworking rooms, have disappeared. To my way of thinking, these subjects provide students with essential life skills. Many young people today live in busy households where both parents are working full-time. As a result, their children are sometimes not learning how to cook a nutritious meal, nor how to mend their clothes, nor how to carry out simple tasks around the home.

Ideally, I would like to see home economics reintroduced into the school curriculum; however, grandparents or an older relative can help fill the gap. They can teach children how to prepare a meal, how to sew up a hem, sew on a button, and plant a small garden, along with learning a few basic woodworking skills. To encourage children, I suggest teaching them how to cook a dozen recipes, then writing up each recipe in an exercise book that can be added to later.

They may discover, as I have done, that cooking is an endlessly fascinating occupation that enriches and celebrates our daily lives.

My mother was fond of saying, 'Through cooking, I show my love for my family and friends.' She taught me a great deal about life: knowledge that I draw upon every day.

Looking back at my life, I think that I have been given a very generous serving. ▪

Peter and I with beer and pasties at Fowey, Cornwall, 2006.

Alison Holst's

All Time
Favourite
Recipes

198 My Mother's Date Scones

199 My Father's Rabbit (or Chicken) Casserole

200 Ginger Fudge

201 Macaroni Mix-up

202 Hash Browns

203 Anne's Oaty Pancakes

204 Stir-fried Pork and Vegetables

206 Lamb Satay

208 Easy 'No Knead' Pizza

210 Cinnamon Oysters

212 Golden Fruit Cake

214 Apple Crumble

215 Savoury Rice

216 Crunchy Lemon Muffins

218 Self-crusting Potato and Vegetable Quiche

220 Chunky Fish Chowder (cooked in a slow cooker)

222 Anne's Stroganoff

My Mother's Date Scones

No one could make scones better than my mother. They melted in your mouth. Sometimes, over a weekend, she'd make six batches, feeding all and sundry.

> 2 cups high grade flour (bread flour)
> – spoon the four into your measuring cup without packing it
> ½ tsp salt
> 2 level Tbsp baking powder
> ½–¾ cup dates (chopped in half)
> 50 g butter (melted)
> ½ cup milk

1. Turn oven to 225°C.
2. Sift dry ingredients into a medium-sized bowl.
3. Add chopped dates.
4. Melt the butter and add the milk, then stir into dry ingredients. Take care not to over-mix. Mixture should be lumpy.
5. Turn dough out onto a floured surface then pat into a rectangle shape (work with dough as lightly as possible). Cut into 6 or 8 square or rectangular scones.
6. Spray some oil onto a baking tray. Place scones closely together on the tray and bake for 10 to 12 minutes, until tops are golden.

My Father's Rabbit (or Chicken) Casserole

My father made this casserole from pieces of bone-in rabbit, chopped in pieces by a butcher, but it is also very good made with boneless chicken thighs.

FOR 4 SERVINGS:

1 Tbsp olive or Canola oil

1 large onion, finely chopped

4 large pieces of bone-in rabbit or boneless chicken thighs

4–8 sprigs of fresh thyme

4–8 fresh sage leaves

4–8 thinly sliced strips of bacon

1½ cups chicken stock

1. Put the oil and the finely chopped onion in a large covered pot or pan and leave it to brown gently while you prepare the rabbit or chicken.
2. Put one or two sprigs of thyme and one or two sage leaves on the outside of each piece of rabbit or chicken, then wrap the bacon round the meat, so the bacon holds the herbs in place.
3. Wrap then knot some string around the bacon-wrapped packages to hold everything in place, or skewer the bacon in place with toothpicks.
4. Push the browned onion aside, add a little extra oil if necessary, then brown the bacon-coated packages, turning them so they colour evenly.
5. Add the chicken stock, cover and cook for about an hour in a 180° oven, until the meat is tender.
6. Discard the pieces of string or the skewers, and serve with mashed potato, some colourful vegetables, and with the thickened pan juices.

Ginger Fudge

Whenever I see a plateful of creamy fudge I think of the times my sweet-toothed sisters and I used to experiment on wet Sunday afternoons.

Fudge-making requires some practice. If you overcook the fudge or overbeat it, you will finish with hard, dry, grainy fudge. A candy thermometer will help.

2 cups sugar
½ cup milk
50 g butter
½–1 tsp ground ginger
1 Tbsp golden syrup
½ tsp vanilla essence

1. Measure the sugar, milk and butter into a medium-sized saucepan. Add the ground ginger and the golden syrup.
2. Bring to the boil over medium heat, stirring occasionally until the mixture starts to boil. Do not stir after the mixture starts boiling.
3. Boil until ¼ tsp of the mixture dropped into cold water forms a soft ball that keeps its roundish shape unless flattened by the fingers, or until a candy thermometer reads 235°F. The fudge is cooked at this stage.
4. Remove from the heat and cool until the saucepan is cool enough to touch. Add the vanilla and beat with a wooden spoon until the fudge shows signs of thickening.
5. Quickly pour the mixture onto a buttered sponge-roll tin, 'swirling' the top with a knife before it sets hard. Cut the fudge into squares as soon as it is firm. (If you have overcooked it, the fudge will harden so that it is difficult to cut neatly.)

Macaroni Mix-up

This tasty one-pan dinner is easy enough for a 'learner' cook to make and ideal for anyone who hates lots of dirty dishes after they cook. This recipe is a dish I used to cook for my flatmates in Auckland.

FOR 4–5 SERVINGS:

1 Tbsp oil

500 g minced beef

1 tsp oreganum

1½ tsp salt

2 tsp sugar

2 cups uncooked macaroni

4 cups boiling water

½ cup tomato paste

3 cups frozen peas or mixed vegetables

1 Heat the oil in a large, non-stick frypan and cook the mince over high heat until it has lost its pinkness, stirring it continuously and breaking up any lumps.

2 Add the oreganum, salt and sugar, then the uncooked macaroni and the boiling water. Stir to mix.

3 Cook with the lid on for 10 minutes, stirring once or twice, and making sure the mixture is bubbling gently but not sticking to the bottom.

4 Stir in the tomato paste and the frozen vegetables, turn up the heat until the mixture starts to boil again, then lower heat, replace the lid, and cook gently for 10 minutes longer. Add more water if the mixture looks dry before the macaroni and vegetables are tender.

5 Serve in bowls, sprinkled with chopped parsley.

Hash Browns

None of our friends in San Francisco could tell me how to make hash browns because they bought theirs frozen (the frozen hash browns had already been par-cooked). They 'crisped' them in a pan until they were golden brown. Here is the recipe that I worked out. It probably isn't authentic, but we all like the end result. It is best to pre-cook potatoes for hash browns several hours before you want to fry them.

1. Scrub two large potatoes.
2. Rub the surface of the potatoes with Canola or olive oil, then put them in a plastic bag. Fold the opening of the bag so it is under the potato.
3. Put the potatoes on opposite sides of the microwave turntable and microwave on High for 8 minutes. For smaller potatoes, cook them for 6 minutes. The centres of the potatoes should be barely cooked.
4. Refrigerate potatoes until they are cold and firm, then grate them coarsely, skin and all, either through the largest holes of a grater, or through the large holed disc of a food processor.
5. Sprinkle grated potato with a little salt and freshly ground black pepper.
6. Put handfuls of potato into a large pan with oil 1 or 2mm deep – or use a smaller pan with oil as above, then sprinkle the shredded potato all over the pan, making one large cake. Don't pack the grated potato too firmly.
7. When cooking the handfuls of potato, turn them when the first side is brown, add a little extra oil if required, then cook the second side.
8. When the large potato cake is golden brown underneath, slide it onto a flat plate, put a little more oil into the pan, and flip the potato cake to cook the other side.
9. When both sides are cooked, cut the hash browns into wedges.

NOTE: If you like these potatoes, microwave large potatoes whenever you think about it. They can be refrigerated for several days.

Anne's Oaty Pancakes

I love these pancakes served for a late weekend breakfast or brunch. Drizzle golden or maple syrup over a pile of two to three pancakes and enjoy!

FOR 2–4 SERVINGS:

¾ cup rolled oats

¾ cup milk

1 egg

½ tsp salt

2–3 Tbsp sugar

½ cup flour

2 tsp baking powder

25 g butter, melted

1. Put the rolled oats into a bowl and pour over the milk.
2. Add the egg, salt and sugar, and beat with a fork until well blended. Sift the flour and baking powder over the mixture, add the melted (but not hot) butter and fold everything together, without over-mixing.
3. Heat a large or electric frypan, and rub a little oil over the surface.
4. Drop spoonfuls of the mixture off the tip of a tablespoon.
5. Turn pancakes, flipping them over when bubbles have formed and burst, and the under-surface is golden brown.
6. Serve several pancakes piled together, with butter and syrup. Serve with bacon or 'skinny' sausages alongside. Good with orange juice, then coffee.

Stir-fried Pork and Vegetables

This is a recipe from the class I attended in Chinatown, San Francisco. There, I made it in a wok over a fierce gas burner, but back in New Zealand I modified the recipe, stir-frying the vegetables in one large pan, and stir-frying the sliced, marinated pork fillet in another, then combining the two together. The two pan method works well and this dish has always been very popular with our family.

FOR 3–4 SERVINGS:

300–400 g pork fillet or another lean pork cut

2 Tbsp sherry

1 Tbsp honey

2 Tbsp soya sauce

4–6 flat mushrooms

1 red pepper

2 zucchinis

¼ to ⅛ drumhead cabbage

3–4 cauli-florets

2 Tbsp canola or other flavourless oil

2 tsp cornflour

3 Tbsp water

1–2 cups of rice

1. Using a sharp knife, cut the pork into thin slices across the grain of the muscle. Cut long strips into smaller strips if necessary. Place the pork in a plastic bag or bowl with the sherry, honey and soya sauce. Mix well and leave to stand while you prepare the vegetables.

2. Cut all the vegetables into slices, then cut crosswise if the strips are too long. They should be bite-sized pieces. Put the prepared vegetables in a large plastic bag and toss them to mix.

3. Both the marinating pork and the vegetables may be refrigerated for several hours. Cook rice to serve with the pork and vegetables before you cook anything else.

4. Heat a large pan so it is very hot, add a tablespoon of the oil then add the prepared vegetables that have been run under a cold tap, then drained.

5. Toss the vegetables in the oil and the steam from the water. If you think the vegetables are not cooking quickly enough, put a lid on the pan for about a minute. Take care not to overcook and soften the vegetables too much — they should be tender-crisp.

6. Heat a smaller pan until very hot, add the remaining tablespoon of oil, then toss the marinated pork in the pan until it is just cooked.

7. Tip the pork into the vegetables; stir to mix everything together.

8. In a cup, stir the cornflour and water together and mix it through the vegetables and pork.

9. Serve immediately on the cooked rice.

Lamb Satay

I hadn't tasted lamb satay until I visited Singapore. It was usually made with tiny cubes of lamb threaded on skewers, with each skewer holding about six cubes, then cooked over a bed of glowing embers.

When we make them at home, I make the cubes 15–20 mm, so there is much more meat on each skewer. You can please yourself which size cubes you prefer — the important thing to remember is not to overcook them.

FOR 4–5 SERVINGS:

500 g of boned lamb shoulder meat, cut in small cubes

2 Tbps Kikkoman soya sauce

2 Tbsp lemon juice

¼ tsp salt

1 Tbsp grated root ginger

1 Tbsp brown sugar

1 Tbsp canola or soya oil

½ tsp turmeric

1 onion, grated

2 cloves garlic, crushed

¼ cup crunchy peanut butter

½ cup coconut milk

Tabasco sauce to taste

1 Thread the cubes of lamb onto bamboo skewers that have been soaked in water. Place on a flat dish.

2 Mix the next 9 ingredients together in a bowl, then brush the mixture over the lamb kebabs and leave to stand for at least 30 minutes.

3 Drain the marinade into a small pot, and simmer it with the peanut butter and coconut milk until thickened to desired consistency.

4 Grill or barbecue the kebabs. The meat should remain pink in the middle.

5 Serve on rice with the sauce poured over top, or serve as finger food with the sauce as a dip.

Easy 'No Knead' Pizza

This is a really quick pizza to make. It takes only about 15 minutes to mix the dough, pat it into a circle and put the toppings of your choice on top. Pop it into a very hot oven and let it cook for 15–20 minutes.

I cup body-temperature water
I tsp yeast
I Tbsp olive oil
I tsp salt
2 tsp sugar
2 cups (275 g) high grade white flour
About ¼ cup extra flour for coating

1 Set oven at 250°C, with a rack above the middle of the oven and a flat metal baking tray on it. (If you have a baking stone, put it in the oven instead of the tray.)
2 Measure the warm water into a large bowl and sprinkle in the yeast, oil, salt and sugar. Mix well until everything is evenly dispersed, then add the first measure of flour (when measuring flour, spoon it lightly into the measuring cup).
3 Mix this to a soft dough with a wooden spoon. The mixture should be soft and slightly sticky. Sprinkle a little of the extra flour over the dough in the bowl and form it into a ball. Leave it to stand while you prepare your choice of topping ingredients. (The dough will start to rise while you do this.)
4 Place a large square of baking paper, or a large non-stick liner, on another flat metal baking tray.

5. Assemble your choice of pizza toppings. Tomatoes and cheese are regarded as essential. Other toppings include mushrooms, olives, onions, basil, salami, pepperoni, red pepper, etc.

6. Return to the dough that should have risen slightly. Sprinkle some of the second measure of flour over the soft pizza dough. Use the spoon to lift the floured dough away from the sides and bottom of the bowl and turn it onto the centre of the baking paper or non-stick liner.

7. With floury hands, first shape the floured dough into a ball, then, using your fingers and hands, pat the ball of dough into a circle 30cm across.

8. Drizzle a little olive oil on the dough and spread it fairly evenly with your fingers over the circle, leaving the outer 2cm uncovered. Add the toppings of your choice, finishing with grated cheese. Fold in the edge of the pizza to make a 1cm rim. Drizzle a little more oil over the topping ingredients.

9. Turn the oven down to 225°C. Open the oven door and carefully slide the pizza, on its baking paper or liner, onto the heated pizza stone or the heated metal tray.

10. Bake for 15–20 minutes until the rim of the pizza is golden brown, then take it from the oven and slide the pizza off the baking paper or liner, onto a cooling rack.

11. Cut into pieces with a knife, rotating cutter or kitchen scissors and serve while warm.

Cinnamon Oysters

Everybody loves cinnamon oysters. They are not difficult to make as long as you measure the ingredients carefully.

FOR 12–18 CINNAMON OYSTERS:

2 large eggs, separated

pinch of salt

½ cup minus 2 Tbsp castor sugar

1 Tbsp golden syrup

½ cup plain flour

1 tsp cinnamon

¼ tsp ground ginger

½ tsp baking soda

1. Heat the oven to 180°C.
2. Beat the egg whites with the salt until foamy. Add the sugar and continue beating until the whites are stiff and the mixture forms peaks with tips that fold over when the beater is lifted from them.
3. Measure the golden syrup using a household spoon. Dip it in hot water, then measure a slightly rounded spoonful. Add the syrup to the whites and beat until well combined. Beat in the egg yolks.
4. Sift together the carefully measured dry ingredients and fold into the egg mixture with a knife or flexible stirrer.
5. Lightly butter or spray shallow patty tins, and spoon in rounded household tablespoons or dessertspoons of the mixture.
6. Bake for 8–10 minutes, or until the centres spring back when lightly pressed. (They will dry out, toughen and shrink if overcooked.) Cool slightly in the patty tins then gently turn them to loosen, or run a knife around the. Cool on a wire rack.

7 Cut through each 'oyster' with a sharp serrated knife, leaving a hinge. They may seem tough and leathery at this stage, but they soften once filled. Fill with plain or vanilla-flavoured, lightly sweetened whipped cream, and leave to stand for about an hour to soften. Freeze at this stage if you prefer. Before serving, dust with sieved icing sugar.

TO FREEZE: Place uncovered on a flat plate or tray in the freezer, until hard, then pack into a container and cover tightly.

Golden Fruit Cake

My recipe for Golden Fruit Cake is Sharon Crosbie's all time favourite cake. She makes about five every Christmas to give to her aunties. Sharon reckons this cake is so delicious that it's enough to make a grown man cry!

The cake is enriched with ground almonds and studded with crystallised fruit.

FOR A 20–23 CM (2.25 KG) CAKE

I cup each of crystallised mango, papaya and pineapple (I suggest buying
   250 g of each crystallised fruit)

2 cups sultanas

I cup chardonnay or other white wine

½–I cup candied cherries (optional)

250 g butter

I cup sugar

5 large eggs

I cup ground almonds

I tsp vanilla

½ tsp almond essence

grated rind of I orange and I lemon

I cup high grade flour

I tsp baking powder

1 Pour boiling water over the mango, papaya and pineapple to soften. Cut into 5 mm cubes with scissors or sharp knife. You'll need at least 3 cups of cubed fruit.

2 Add washed sultanas.

3. Simmer fruit and wine in covered pan for 5 minutes or till all liquid is absorbed.
4. Spread fruit out in a roasting pan to cool and to soak up remaining liquid.
5. Leave for several hours or overnight then stir in cherries.
6. In a large bowl, beat sugar and softened (but not melted) butter till creamy. Beat in 1 egg at a time, adding a spoonful of almonds with each. Then beat in essences, remaining almonds and citrus rind.
7. Add the sifted flour and baking powder. Use your hand to mix in the cold prepared fruit.
8. Spread mixture in a lined tin.
9. Bake below middle of oven at 150°C for 45 minutes then lower temperature to 130°C for 2 hours. (Lower 10°C if using fan bake.)
10. Bake until skewer comes out clean.
11. When cool, wrap, and refrigerate until used. (Leave at least one week before cutting.)

Apple Crumble

Peter grows apples at Manakau and this is one of our favourite desserts. It's much quicker to make a crumbled topping than to make pastry and in our house the crumble rates just as high as a pie.

The leftovers, warmed in the oven and served with yoghurt, make a good breakfast.

I grate the apples, skin and all, instead of peeling then slicing the fruit. It gives a fresher flavour to the crumble.

FOR 4 SERVINGS:
½ cup flour
½ tsp cinnamon
½ tsp mixed spice
¾ cup sugar
75 g butter
½ cup rolled oats
4 medium-sized apples

1 Measure the flour, spices and sugar into a medium-sized bowl or food processor. Cut or rub in the butter until crumbly, then add the rolled oats.
2 Grate the unpeeled apples into a shallow medium-sized ovenware dish.
3 Sprinkle the crumbly topping evenly over the apples.
4 Bake at 190°C for 45 minutes, until the topping is golden brown. Serve hot or warm with cream or ice-cream.

Savoury Rice

Once I started cooking rice in my microwave oven, I stopped cooking it any other way. Microwaved rice does not cook dramatically quickly, because it needs time to soak up the liquid, but it has other important advantages.

It needs no attention while it cooks or after cooking. It doesn't burn on the bottom or need draining afterwards.

It's easy to reheat, without needing additions — in fact it may be cooked, served, refrigerated and reheated in the same dish. Its flavour is excellent and the yield large. I hope you will now be tempted to microwave other grains too.

FOR 4 SERVINGS:

25 g butter or oil

1 onion, finely chopped

1–2 garlic cloves, chopped

¼–½ cup finely chopped celery or red or green pepper

1 cup long grain rice

2 cups very hot water

½ tsp salt

2–4 Tbsp chopped parsley

1. Heat butter or oil and vegetables in a covered, 2 litre microwave casserole dish, on High (100% power) for 3 minutes, stirring after 1 minute.
2. Add the rice, stir well and cook for 2 minutes longer.
3. Add the hot water and salt, cover and cook for 12 minutes.
4. Leave to stand for 5 minutes, then stir in the chopped parsley and serve.

Crunchy Lemon Muffins

Everybody at our house rates these muffins highly. The sugar and lemon juice drizzled over the top, after baking, give a tangy flavour and an interesting sugary crunch.

FOR 12 MUFFINS:

2 cups self-raising flour

¾ cup sugar

75 g butter

1 cup milk

1 egg

grated rind of 1 large or 2 small lemons

Topping:

¼ cup lemon juice

¼ cup sugar

1. Measure the flour and sugar into a bowl and toss to mix.
2. Melt the butter, add the milk, egg and lemon rind and beat well with a fork to combine. Add this mixture to the dry ingredients and combine only until the dry ingredients have been lightly dampened but not thoroughly mixed.
3. Divide the mixture evenly between 12 medium-sized muffin pans that have been well coated with a non-stick spray (oil).

4. Bake at 200°C for 10 minutes or until lightly browned.
5. Stir together the lemon juice and sugar topping without dissolving the sugar, and drizzle this over the hot muffins as soon as they are removed from the oven. Leave to stand in the pans for only a few minutes after this, in case the syrup hardens as it cools and sticks the muffins to the pans. If this happens, it may be necessary to use a knife to 'lever' the muffins from the pan. Take care not to damage the pan's non-stick finish.
6. Serve with lightly whipped cream and fresh fruit or berries.

Self-crusting Potato and Vegetable Quiche

Self-crusting quiches are made without pastry crusts but form their own fairly firm outer layers as they cook.

For best results you need to remember these points:

- Use a metal pie plate or flan tin with a solid (not push-out) base.
- Use a non-stick finish.
- Lightly oil or butter the dish before use, regardless of the finish.
- Take care not to over-mix the egg mixture when you add the flour or it may not form two layers as it cooks.
- Bake at a high temperature so the crust browns well.
- Leave to stand for 5 minutes after removing from the oven, before turning out.

FOR 4–6 SERVINGS:

1 large onion, chopped

2 garlic cloves

1 Tbsp butter

3 eggs

¾ tsp salt

1 cup milk

½ cup self-raising flour

2 cooked potatoes

1 cup drained cooked asparagus, spinach, mushrooms or broccoli

1 cup grated tasty cheese

1. Cook the chopped onion and garlic in butter until tender. Cool. Stir in the eggs, salt and milk, and beat with fork until mixed.
2. Pour this mixture into a large bowl containing the flour, and stir with a fork until just combined. Add the potatoes cut in 1 cm cubes, the chopped, well-drained vegetables and cheese.
3. Pour into a prepared 20–23 cm pan. Garnish with sliced tomato or thinly sliced red and green peppers. Bake at 220°C for 20–30 minutes, until lightly browned and set in the centre.

Chunky Fish Chowder (cooked in a slow cooker)

Chowder is really a 'sloppy' stew or a very chunky soup. Served with crusty bread and a salad, it's a satisfying main meal. The onion and potato are essential ingredients, but you can leave out some of the other vegetables if you prefer. Chowder can be left on LOW or KEEP WARM in the slow cooker for late arriving guests.

FOR ABOUT 6 LARGE SERVINGS:

1 large onion
2 large cloves garlic
2 tsp oil or butter
2 fairly large potatoes
1 large carrot
2 cups cubed pumpkin, optional
1 cup cubed (inner) celery stalks
2 cups hot tap water
2 tsp instant stock powder (fish, chicken or vegetable)
1 x 440 g can of any light-coloured cream soup; e.g. celery, chicken, mushroom or onion
1 x 440 g can creamed corn
about 500 g raw, skinless, boneless fish fillets
½ cup milk powder
chopped parsley or dill leaves

1. Turn the slow cooker on to HIGH and coat it with non-stick spray.
2. Cut the onions into 2 cm squares and finely chop the garlic. Mix with the oil or melted butter, and cook until transparent in a non-stick pan on the stove, then put them in the slow cooker bowl.
3. Scrub or peel potatoes, then cut into 1 cm cubes. Add to the onion mixture in the slow cooker bowl. Chop the carrots, pumpkin and the celery stalks into slightly smaller pieces and add to the potato and onion mixture.
4. Add the hot water and stock powder (or cubes), then stir in the can of soup (regular or concentrated) and the creamed corn. Put on the lid and cook on HIGH for 3–4 hours, or until all the vegetables are tender.
5. Cut the fish into 15 mm cubes, then stir them into the chowder and cook on HIGH for 1 hour longer. Mix the milk and powdered milk together until smooth, then stir into the soup. Leave for 15 minutes longer, then adjust seasonings and serve sprinkled with fresh parsley or dill leaves.

VARIATIONS: Thaw frozen (precooked) prawns, and add with whole or halved smoked mussels half an hour before serving. Creamy Vegetable Chowder is made by leaving the fish out of this recipe.

Anne's Stroganoff

This is an excellent recipe to make ahead and serve when entertaining a family with children.

FOR 8 SERVINGS:

250 g small lasagna noodles or other pasta shapes

50 g butter

2 large onions, chopped

2 cloves garlic, chopped

about 300 g button mushrooms, quartered

1 kg minced beef or lamb

1 packet (30 g) mushroom soup mix

2 cups water, or ½ cup white wine and 1½ cups water

2 Tbsp tomato paste

1 carton sour cream

about 1 tsp salt

about ¼ cup Parmesan cheese

1. Cook the pasta in plenty of boiling, salted water until barely tender. Drain, rinse with cold water (to stop it cooking) and spread in a large, shallow, lightly sprayed ovenware dish.

2. While the pasta cooks, melt the butter in a large frypan and cook the onions, garlic and mushrooms until the onions are transparent. Remove from the pan then brown the mince until it has lost all its pinkness. Stir in the soup mix, then add the water (or wine and water) and stir until the mixture boils. Simmer for 5 minutes, then mix in the onion mixture, tomato paste and sour cream. Taste and add salt as needed to bring out flavour.

3 Spoon the mixture over the pasta (it will soak up some of the sauce later). Sprinkle with Parmesan cheese, cover and refrigerate until needed.

4 To cook, cover and bake at 180°C for 20 minutes, then bake uncovered for another 20 minutes, or until the mixture has heated right through and is bubbling around the edges. Serve with a crisp, green salad.

Appendix **one:**

Margaret Payne's Memoirs

The following is an extract from my mother's memoir,
which she wrote in January 1973.

Alison has asked me to try and write a record of our family life. It is difficult to know where to begin!

Just snatches of mother's childhood come to me: she told us of finding 'goodies' on the beach in Kent after a shipwreck. She found a small, star-shaped brooch and mother used to wear it on a black, velvet band round her neck. She also remembered a train journey alone, as a very small girl, with a ticket on a string around her neck to indicate her destination!

My father, William James Dickie, met my mother's brothers on the West Coast of the South Island, where they were goldmining. Her brothers asked her to come to New Zealand from England to join them, because they needed a housekeeper. William's father had died early, so Dad helped his mother, working in her drapery business. He had one sister, Lillias, and also three brothers, I think.

Dad and Mother were married and they went over to Canterbury to live, as Dad had decided to be a farmer. They had a three-roomed house set in a 500 acre field — with no trees and absolutely no garden. At that time, the Canterbury plains were subjected to terrific nor'westers, since there were no plantations to break the force of the wind.

As the years rolled on, my parents built a home at Somerton. They planted trees and shelter belts, and life progressed. My brothers Beacon and Colin were born here, as well as Nellie (Mary Ellen) — there were two years between each child. Then the bomb fell — Dad got a good offer for the property, and the place was sold.

It nearly broke Mother's heart at leaving this place, she said. Dad finally bought a property of about 800 acres at Lyndhurst, called 'Ardagh'. He bought it from Mr Holmes, who had given it this name because they came from Ireland.

I believe I was called Margaret after an aunt who arrived at the house unexpectedly, and helped to deliver me — I came too early. My father was away and others were at school, and Mother told me later that when she heard the buggy and horses arriving she sent up a prayer of thankfulness.

A few memorable stories still make me smile. The Vicar was given permission by our father to use our donkey to teach his daughter to ride. Dad didn't consult with my brothers ('the boys' as we called them) and they decided that no parson was getting their means of transport. So when the Vicar arrived with his daughter for a demonstration ride the animal behaved abominably. The boys had put a wee piece of gorse under the saddle so when someone sat on the saddle, it hurt the animal and he bucked and played up generally. Far too unsafe an animal to allow any Vicar's daughter to use!

The school teacher boarded with us for a few months each year. I realise now what a good sport she was, for we were just shocking to her!

She told Mother she'd like to try and do all the things on a farm that other people did, so we decided we'd teach her! And we began by milking cows, giving her the one that kicked most, and behaved badly. We'd place her strategically in the middle of the cowshed and then we'd squirt her with milk from either side. Up she'd jump and the cow would start misbehaving.

And she wanted to learn how to swim in the pool too, and we'd all duck her and she didn't ever tell on us! How we loved it!

We loved our ponies, the jersey cow, and 'Soldier' the black Cocker spaniel.

A naturalist, Tom Hall, used our home as a place to call, and helped us in our love of nature. He was a collector of moths and butterflies and how we loved his visits.

Another thing we looked forward to was the visit of a van owned by Assyrians, Mr and Mrs Farrah. They travelled the countryside in their caravan drawn by an old horse. They sold all sorts of drapery and we adored, after tea, being allowed to view their wares — cottons, beads, materials, wools, bangles and brooches.

Mrs Farrah was a good cook too, and mother allowed her to use the stove. She'd make intriguing dishes — meat, rice and veggies — wrapped up in cabbage leaves, with plenty of oil.

The arrival of the Chaff Cutter to get chaff for horses was an event, but the cutter never stayed long. It was the threshing machine we loved most, for besides the engine and the threshing machine there was a cookhouse and a whare for the men to sleep in.

The cooks coped wonderfully well to produce good meals for hungry harvesters. It was often noted, too, that our fruit orchard and vegetable garden became depleted after these visits. Shearing time was a busy time too, as shearers began with early morning tea at 5 a.m., breakfast at 7:30 a.m., morning tea near 10 a.m., dinner 12:30 p.m., afternoon tea at about 3:30 p.m. and tea in the evening being a moveable feast, depending on the work done and the weather. There were sheep ticks too — we loathed them!

Feeding calves and pet lambs and pigs was fun. The greedy calves would become so anxious to gobble up their food they'd get the handle of the bucket stuck over their heads. The lambs were sweet but greedy too, and many were the bottles of milk we fed them. Getting the lamb cheque was a great event, believe me! Once we housed six lambs in an empty garage, and one got into some spilt paint — Paddle we called him.

We always had five to six miles to drive to school, and catching a pony in the dark winter mornings, grooming him and feeding him before we started off, was no enviable task.

I remember so well when the telephone was first installed at Ardagh. There was a party line of about six houses, and each home had a different ring. Some families took up residence beside the phone and listened to all that was said. You'd hear the eavesdropper listening to our conversations, but telling the children to be quiet so they could hear it all! That's truly how 'bush telephones' began!

Music lessons were a big part of our lives. Sunday nights at Ardagh were quite a joy, the piano would be playing, a crowd would be singing, and the odd violinist would be there — or an accordion player. These were nights to remember, and always about ten to fifteen sat down around the table to tea on Sunday evenings. The cooking for this was done by Mother and the girls of the family.

A grass tennis court at Ardagh was a boon to us as children, and we loved the big garden where mother had a garden party each November. This was a big event. Much baking was done, the lawn edges were neatened, all the weeds were banished and the yards swept clean, besides much polishing in the house. All the church people congregated and it was such fun to remember.

The first motor car we had was a Flanders, then a Hupmobile and then a Buick!

Dad and the boys always did the driving, and we were never encouraged in this line.

Colin, the second eldest son, was a splendid baker but we girls hated
him to be in the kitchen, turning out such creditable cooking, and then
being praised. We, as females, felt it was offensive to our dignity. And need
I add, we did many nasty things to ensure many of those cakes didn't rise
—for example, opening the oven door a bit, or failing to keep the stove
stoked, all not very nice traits, you'll agree!

Dad's entry into Parliament for the Selwyn electorate gave him eight
busy years—busy ones for mother, too, as she had to cope with us and
the farm, while he was engaged in parliamentary business in Wellington.

We had exciting holidays going to Wellington in session time. Mother
always made us go to bed as soon as we got onto the Lyttelton–Wellington
ferry, and because of this, we were seldom sea-sick.

I well remember one of the first trans-Tasman phone calls being made
as my uncle, J.R. Smith, a former engineer, was working with something
to do with broadcasting. Dad, being then a Member of Parliament, was
selected as the person to receive this call. What excitement too!

Some very fine people shared the life at Ardagh with us, and the
children of these people grew up with us, and came to our schools. When,
later on, it was decided to have just a male cook rather than a 'married
couple', in the cottage, the conditions changed. It became more a men's
world and our frequent visits to the cottage were stopped.

Mother used to visit the male cook periodically, to discuss what
was needed. These male cooks were a mixed bag, though. I recall with
amusement the one mother caught putting a shine on his scones, using
his shaving brush!

Another made the most beautiful pies with lovely pastry and the most
ornamental edgings. The men were loud in their praises of his culinary
skills but their enthusiasm diminished somewhat when Mother found

he (the cook) managed to get his 'extra nice trimmings' by indenting the pastry at the edges with his own false teeth!

The farm at Ardagh was run by the family while Dad was away, but after Dad's untimely death, it had to be sold at a great loss, and mother went to live in the small country town of Methven. By then Beacon, Colin and Nell were married and away from home. Allan kept on the land, and I began teaching, but later turned to nursing in Christchurch Hospital.

I forgot to mention that Mother and Dad brought up two more children, Gertie and Albert Dent, as their parents had died. They were cousins of Dad's.

Mother was a woman with a great faith, and believe me, she needed it, to carry her over the difficult times. The Depression was so awful to live through that she often wondered where food and clothes for us would come from. I remember her driving a horse and cart over twenty miles to Ashburton to supply eggs to the grocer and in return, get the needed groceries for a growing family.

The boys had to help mend our shoes, and dear old Mother, always a good sewer, would make us dresses and coats out of anything that came to hand. She was always ready to help others too, and offer hospitality to many.

Near the time of Mother's demise, her brother, still in Cobden, was very ill too. He wanted one of us to go over to the West Coast as he was near his end. He'd refused even to open the letters and photos that Mother had sent him of us when babies, but he wanted some blood relatives at his death. We couldn't go, though, for our allegiance was to Mother. They died within a day of one another! ▪

Me with Simon and Kirsten when Food without Fuss *was published, 1972.*

100
cookbook titles from
1966–2011

1
1966
Here's How
HICKS SMITH

2
1967
Meals with the Family
HICKS SMITH

3
1972
Food Without Fuss
METHUEN

4
1974
The New Zealand
Radio and Television
Cookbook
HAMLYN

5
1974
More Food Without Fuss
HICKS SMITH

6
1975
Simply Delicious
HICKS SMITH

7
1976
Lamb for all Seasons
HICKS SMITH

8
1978
What's Cooking?
INL

9
1978
Kitchen Diary 1
INL

10
1979
Kitchen Diary 2
INL

11
1980
Alison Holst's Food
Processor Book
INL

12
1980
Kitchen Diary 3
INL

13

1981

Kitchen Diary 4

INL

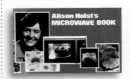

14

1982

Alison Holst's
Microwave Book

INL

15

1982

Kitchen Diary 5

INL

16

1982

Let's Cook

INL

21

1984

Let's Cook Some More

INL

22

1985

Kitchen Diary 8

INL

23

1986

Cooking Class 1

BECKETTS

24

1986

Kitchen Diary 9

INL

29

1987

New Zealand Recipe
Notes

BATEMAN

30

1988

Cooking Class 3

BECKETTS

31

1988

Kitchen Diary 11

INL

32

1989

Microwave Menus 1

CJPUBLISHING

17
1983
Kitchen Diary 6
INL

18
1984
Alison Holst Cooks
BECKETTS

19
1984
Dollars and Sense
INL

20
1984
Kitchen Diary 7
INL

25
1987
Cooking Class 2
BECKETTS

26
1987
Family Cookbook
METHUEN

27
1987
Kitchen Diary 10
INL

28
1987
Lambtastic
BYERS & ASSOCIATES

33
1989
Complete Cooking Class
BECKETTS

34
1989
Kitchen Diary 12
INL

35
1989
Microwave Menus 2
CJPUBLISHING

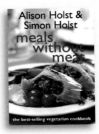

36
1990
Meals Without Meat*
NEW HOLLAND

* with Simon Holst

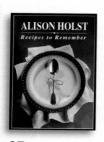

37

1990

Recipes to Remember
BYERS & ASSOCIATES

38

1991

Microwave Menus
1 & 2
CJPUBLISHING

39

1991

Barbecue Cooking
GAS

40

1991

Best of Alison Holst
CJPUBLISHING

45

1991

New Microwave
Cookbook
BECKETTS

46

1992

Mini-Money Meals
INL

47

1992

New Kitchen Diary 2
INL

48

1993

Family Favourites
CJPUBLISHING

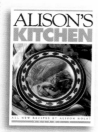

53

1995

Alison's Kitchen
INL

54

1995

Cooking for Christmas
HYNDMAN

55

1995

Food for Young Families
PENGUIN

56

1995

Best Potato Recipes
HYNDMAN

* with Simon Holst

41

1991

Best of Home Cooking

CJPUBLISHING

42

1991

Food for Healthy Appetites

GAS

43

1991

Kitchen Diary Collection

INL

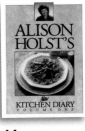

44

1991

New Kitchen Diary 1

INL

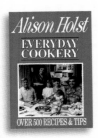

49

1993

Everyday Cookery

BECKETTS

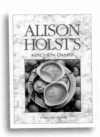

50

1993

New Kitchen Diary 3

INL

51

1994

Breakfasts and Brunches

CJPUBLISHING

52

1994

Marvellous Muffins

HYNDMAN

57

1995

Good Food

CJPUBLISHING

58

1996

Meals Without Red Meat

CJPUBLISHING

59

1996

Alison's Kitchen 2

INL

60

1996

Chocolate Temptations

HYNDMAN

61

1996

Sausage Book

HYNDMAN

62

1997

Bread Book*

HYNDMAN

63

1997

Dollars and Sense:
Eating Well For Less

CJPUBLISHING

64

1997

More Marvellous
Muffins*

HYNDMAN

69

1998

Very Easy Vegetarian*

NEW HOLLAND

70

1999

School Lunches and
After School Snacks*

HYNDMAN

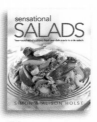

71

1999

Sensational Salads

HYNDMAN
Simon

72

1999

Best Ever Muffins/Breads
Biscuits/Slices & More*

HYNDMAN

77

2001

More for Less
Cookbook*

HYNDMAN

78

2001

Quick & Easy Twenty
Minute Meals*

HYNDMAN

79

2001

Quick & Easy Twenty
Minute Starters*

HYNDMAN

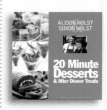

80

2001

Quick & Easy Twenty
Minute Desserts*

HYNDMAN

* with Simon Holst

65

1997

Soup Book

HYNDMAN

66

1998

Best Baking*

HYNDMAN

67

1998

Best Mince
Recipes

HYNDMAN

68

1998

Children's Step-by-Step
Fun-to-Cook Book

HYNDMAN

73

2000

Really Easy
Chicken Recipes*

HYNDMAN

74

2000

Baby Food and
Beyond*

HYNDMAN

75

2000

Healthy and
Delicious Muffins*

HYNDMAN

76

2000

Ultimate
Collection

NEW HOLLAND

81

2003

100 Favourite Muffins
& Slices*

HYNDMAN

82

2003

Alison's Pantry

ALISON HOLST

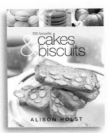

83

2004

100 Favourite Cakes
& Biscuits*

HYNDMAN

84

2004

100 Favourite Twenty
Minute Dishes*

HYNDMAN

85

2006

100 Great Ways to
use Slow Cookers &
Crockpots*

HYNDMAN

86

2006

Food To Go*

HYNDMAN

87

2006

Cool Food for
Warmer Days*

HACHETTE LIVRE

88

2006

New Zealand
Diabetes Cookbook*

HYNDMAN

93

2009

Marvellous Mince &
Sensational Sausages*

HYNDMAN

94

2009

Fast & Fun Family Food

PENGUIN

95

2009

New Zealand
Barbecue Book*

HYNDMAN

96

2010

New Zealand
Bread Book*

HYNDMAN

* with Simon Holst

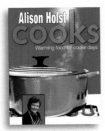

89

2006

Warming Food
for Cooler Days

HACHETTE LIVRE

90

2007

Year-Round Ways to
use Slow Cookers &
Crockpots*

HYNDMAN

91

2008

Popular Potatoes*

HYNDMAN

92

2008

Kiwi Favourites*

HYNDMAN

97

2010

100 Favourite Ways
With Chicken*

HYNDMAN

98

2010

My Own Kiwi
Favourites*

BATEMAN

99

2011

Delicious Slow
Cooker Recipes*

HYNDMAN

100

2011

Home-grown
Cook

HYNDMAN

Here's How

COOKING WITH
Alison Holst

ALISON HOLST'S

KITCHEN DIARY
VOLUME 12

Alison Holst's
New Zealand
Recipe
Notes

alison holst
MORE
FOOD WITHOUT FUSS

Marvellous
muffins
ALISON HOLST

MEALS with the family

by
Alison Holst

LAMB FOR ALL SEASONS
Recipes selected and edited by
ALISON HOLST

Alison Holst
what's
COOKING

New Alison Holst's
MICROWAVE COOKBOOK

Alison Holst's
KITCHEN DIARY
Volume 8

ALISON HOLST

Food
without fuss

Alison Holst
COOKS

AS SEEN ON
TELEVISION

ALISON HOLST'S

KITCHEN
DIARY
Volume 11

Alison Holst's
Complete
Cooking
Class

ALL THREE BOOKS
FROM THE
TELEVISION SERIES

10TH ANNIVERSARY
ALISON HOLST'S
Kitchen Diary

'Lambtastic

Quick Microwave
and Frypan Recipes
Edited by
Alison Holst

ALISON HOLST
SIMPLY
DELICIOUS

Let's Cook Some More
with Alison Holst

TVNZ
ENTERPRISES

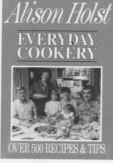

Alison Holst
EVERYDAY
COOKERY

OVER 500 RECIPES & TIPS

Let's Cook Some More
with Alison Holst

TVNZ
ENTERPRISES

THE NEW ZEALAND
RADIO & TELEVISION
COOKBOOK

EDITED BY
ALISON HOLST

Let's Cook
with Alison Holst

Alison Holst's
KITCHEN DIARY
Volume 6

Alison Holst's
MICROWAVE BOOK

COOKING WITH
ALISON
HOLST
BARBECUE
COOKING

BBQ
FACTORY

Alison Holst's
KITCHEN DIARY
Volume 5

ALISON HOLST'S
a book of
seasonal recipes
KITCHEN DIARY

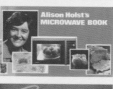

Alison Holst
COOKS

AS SEEN ON
TELEVISION

ALISON HOLST'S
Food processor book

Alison Holst's
KITCHEN DIARY
Volume 7

Alison Holst's
KITCHEN DIARY
Volume 4

Alison Holst's
Dollars
and Sense
COOKBOOK

REVISED EDITION

Alison Holst's
Cooking
Class
Book II

BASED ON
THE NEW ZEALAND TELEVISION SERIES